The Young Person's Guide
to Playing the Piano

THE YOUNG PERSON'S GUIDE TO PLAYING THE PIANO

Sidney Harrison

FABER AND FABER LIMITED

3 Queen Square

London

First edition 1966
Second edition 1973
Published by
Faber and Faber Limited
3 Queen Square London WC1
Printed in Great Britain by
Whitstable Litho
All rights reserved

ISBN 0 571 04787 4

Contents

I. A Piano is a Piano   *page* 9

II. The Beauty of the Thing   15

III. Friend or Foe   17

IV. Looking at Music   19

V. Phrasing and Pedalling   24

VI. The Use of Your Self   28

VII. More About Fingers   33

VIII. Relaxation   37

IX. The Beauty-of-Tone Problem   40

X. The Design Problem   46

XI. How to Practise   52

XII. Playing With All You've Got   57

XIII. Accompanying   62

XIV. Pianos and Pianists as They Used to Be   64

XV. Heavy Pianists, Light Pianists, and Jazz Pianists   67

XVI. Interpretation and the Unlearning of Rules   70

Contents

XVII. THE INTERPRETATION OF TIME   *page* 80

XVIII. THE HARPSICHORD PROBLEM   85

XIX. THE SONATA PROBLEM   89

XX. THE AGE OF SONG   91

XXI. STRENGTH AND AGILITY   93

XXII. TAKE A BOW   96

INDEX   99

I

A Piano is a Piano

How would you describe a piano?

Is it a string instrument? Well, it certainly has strings but it does not belong to the same family as violins and 'cellos. Is it a percussion instrument? Yes, I suppose so if you think of the hammers hitting the wires, yet a piano is not much like a drum or a gong. Is it anything like a harp? Perhaps it is. If you look inside a piano at the strings stretched across the iron frame you certainly see something like a harp; but whereas harp strings are plucked, piano strings are briskly banged.

Obviously a piano is a keyboard instrument and therefore something like an organ or a harpsichord, but you have only to touch all three instruments to see how different they are.

A piano is a piano.

*   *   *

A piano is a sort of one-man band. It can play up to ten notes at once, high or low, loud or soft. It can match its strength against a large orchestra or play a duet with just one violin. It never really blends with any other sound yet it accompanies the voice with surprising success. It even manages to disguise its one great limitation. It pretends to produce a singing tone though you and I know that each note starts with a bump of sound and then proceeds to die away.

The box of steel wires and busy hammers we call a *pianoforte* ought, by

9

the look of it, to be a soulless contraption, but in fact it can be so expressive that it has had more romantic music composed for it than any other instrument in existence.

Of course you must know how to persuade and command the piano, but the first thing is to fall in love with it. Then it will persuade and command you, and you will never feel that spending time with your best friend is mere work or duty. For my part I fell in love with the piano at the age of four and have never fallen out of love. I give my heart to the piano much as a puppeteer gives his heart to his doll. We know we are operating machines but. . . .

However, let us look at the machine.

You know the outside of a piano. You know the way the keys, black and white, are arranged on the keyboard. You know that the keyboard can be hidden under its own lid called a 'fall'. Now let us look inside. You may not be very interested in the works of your piano but you must surely be a little curious about what happens when you press a key and get a sound.

First of all look at the strings. The lower the longer; the higher the shorter. On the far left we have the longest of all. It is bound round with copper wire for strength and weight. Weight, like length, produces low pitch. However, for a good sound the string must be stretched tight, and stretching raises the pitch. Problem: how high should a low note be tuned?

When you play the lowest notes each hammer hits one string. Higher up you find that a hammer hits two strings at once—two strings to compensate for the fact that shorter strings produce weaker sounds that die sooner. Still further up, each hammer strikes three strings (not copper bound). After that there isn't room for more strings per note: we must make do with three.

On most pianos the lowest strings are stretched diagonally to gain a few extra inches of length. For this to be possible they must be placed at a different level. One batch of strings crosses above the others. The piano is then described as overstrung. Before over-stringing was invented pianos were straight-strung, and straight-stringing is still occasionally found on cheap uprights.

While defining technical terms let us agree that horizontal strings belong to grand pianos: vertical strings to uprights. The expression 'upright grand' is only an advertiser's phrase.

Play a note. The hammer strikes the strings, the strings vibrate, and vibration travels through the air to your ears. The vibration travels: the air doesn't. There is no wind blowing out of the piano.

The vibration of the string is communicated to the soundboard. This is a plank of wood, behind the strings on an upright, below them on a grand. This vibrates 'in sympathy' and makes the sound richer. However, as we never get anything for nothing, we pay a price. Some of the energy that the hammer puts into the string is stolen from the string by the soundboard. What we gain in richness we lose in duration. A string without a soundboard would actually vibrate a little longer but not half so agreeably.

You will notice that a hammer is not pushed against the strings. It is flung or thrown and it rebounds smartly like a ball thrown against a wall even though you may be holding the key down. The key stays down but the hammer does not stay up. How is this managed?

What happens is this: the key itself is a see-saw. You push the visible end and the other end goes up. If you look at the illustration (Fig. 1) you will see a rod (d) pushing the piece of felt near the hinge of the hammer. This remains in contact for about half the distance. It then slides to one side and the hammer completes its journey by momentum. This arrangement is called the escapement.

Playing the note you are hardly aware of this. The mechanism—the 'action'—is designed to give you the feeling that pushing the key down to its bed is the same thing as pushing the hammer up to its string.

The hammer starts the vibration. The hammer's rebound allows the vibration to continue. So does something else. Lying on every string except the very high ones there is a pad of felt called a damper. If it stayed there, no vibration could occur. However, when you strike a key, the damper rises and is held off the vibrating string while you hold the key down. When you release the key, the damper falls and damps out the vibration. The cycle of operations is complete.

The situation is not so simple if you press the right pedal. This holds all the dampers off the strings. Taking your hand off the keys no longer

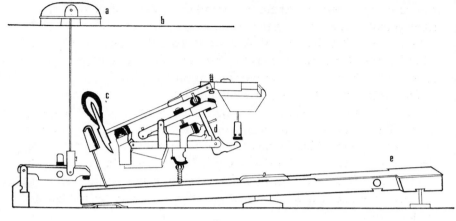

FIG. I

Figures 1 and 2 represent a side view of the action of one note on a grand piano.

A key is like a seesaw. Press the visible end down and the other end goes up. In Figure 1 the key (e) is up. The hammer (c) is at rest. The damper (a) lies on the string (b) preventing any vibration. The rod (d) can be thought of as a sort of finger; and the finger tip is hidden in a slot in the cross piece. This finger tip touches the round piece of felt above it.

In Figure 2 the key has been pushed down. The other end of the seesaw goes up and, through a vertical rod, takes the damper off the string. At the same time the force is communicated to the 'finger' (d) which pushes the piece of felt. This pushes the hammer-shank, and the hammer (c) is on its way towards the string. But now the 'finger-tip' slips to one side of the piece of felt, escaping from its original position. The hammer flies the rest of the way by momentum. It is not pushed against the string: it is thrown at the string, from which it bounces back. It is the escapement that makes this possible. The 'finger' of the escapement, in fact, flicks the hammer. (Piano-action makers call this 'finger' a hopper.)

The damper stays off the string so long as the key is held down (or so long as the sustaining pedal is down).

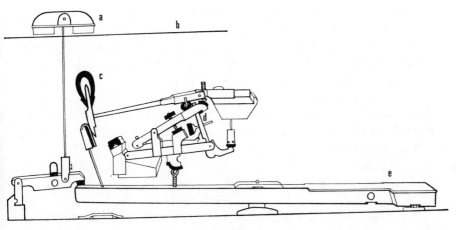

FIG. 2

The drawings are of a Schwander action manufactured by Messrs Herrburger, Brooks, Ltd., of Long Eaton.

stops the sound. To stop the sound you must release the pedal (but keep your foot in contact otherwise you will make pedal noises).

You have only to experiment with this 'sustaining pedal' to realize why children nearly always call it the loud pedal, even though artists use it for soft music. You had better learn to use it well (just how will be discussed later) because bad pedalling can damage your playing disastrously.

The other pedal, the soft pedal, produces its effect in one of two ways. On most uprights it brings the hammers nearer the strings, reduces the fling of the hammer to 'half-throw', and thereby produces less sound. It also slightly alters the feel of the action and is disliked by concert artists. On grand pianos the soft pedal causes the whole of the action, including the keyboard, to slide slightly to one side. This means that a hammer normally hitting three strings now hits two. In the double string region it hits one. In the deep bass the one string is hit slightly off centre.

If the composer writes *una corda* (one string) in the copy he means soft pedal. For normal working after an *una corda* passage he writes *tre corde* (three strings). This is unscientific but we know what he means.

You will sometimes see three pedals on a piano. On a big Steinway concert-grand the middle pedal will give you a selective sustaining effect.

You can play a low octave, say, and sustain it with the middle pedal. All other notes are unaffected by this pedal. Play the desired notes first, pedal them while the keys are down, and then take your hands off. There is a cheap substitute for this: a middle pedal that sustains all the bass notes up to middle-C.

On very old uprights the left pedal produced its effect by placing a ribbon of felt between the hammers and the strings. The effect was absurdly muffled, but it was useful for people who wanted to practise without annoying the neighbours.

*   *   *

If a pupil asks 'Is it necessary to understand the machinery of a piano?', I am a little taken aback. There is no need to be a piano-mechanic, but how can a pianist bear to be totally ignorant of his instrument? Furthermore we need to know why a fine concert-grand can cost ten times as much as a little domestic upright. (Yes, I did say ten times.)

Without this knowledge people deceive themselves into thinking that some beat-up collection of old iron and timber, full of worm, moth, rust, and dust, is one of the 'good old makes such as you don't get nowadays'. Or a town council will build a new hall for a million pounds and furnish it with a second-hand piano. And some teachers, who ought to know better, instruct their pupils to make meaningless hand and finger actions because they do not understand what actually happens inside a piano.

II

The Beauty of the Thing

While we are inspecting pianos let us compare an expensive concert-grand with a domestic upright. Notice the size of the soundboard and take the great maker's word for it that it is a carefully selected piece of slowly seasoned wood. Observe the length of the bass strings. They had better be very good strings for they will have to be stretched very tight indeed to come up to the right pitch. And the iron frame will have to be suitably strong to stand the strain.

Unfortunately it is impossible to lengthen high strings to the same degree. A very long piano sometimes gets a little out of proportion—the bass too strong for the treble.

As for beauty of tone, this depends on certain vibrations over and above the ones that create the recognized pitch. A string does not vibrate in a simple to-and-fro movement. It comes to life in a complex shiver. This produces the expected note at the right pitch plus a faint chord of other, higher notes called overtones or harmonics or partials. You do not consciously hear them: they are secret ingredients in the flavour of the note. All instruments have these overtones, but in varying proportions; which is why a piano, a trumpet, or a violin may all play the 'same' A, but you know which is playing. (By the way, the 'tuning A' given by the oboe to the orchestra should have a vibration frequency of 440 per second.)

Part of the joy of playing a fine, big piano is sheer volume. There is also the kind of softness that carries to the back of a large hall. A fine piano welcomes a plunge of fingers on to a fortissimo chord that on a small piano or a baby grand would produce a tinny tinkle or a dull thud.

But tone is not everything. As you make more and more demands in the way of speed and agility you need a fine, responsive action. This enables you to control the variety and contrast of loudness and softness. The effect will be a beauty of sound that cannot be demonstrated by just playing one specimen chord. A few specimen chords can flatter a cheap piano, but try playing a concerto on it.

When buying a piano, always get something bigger and better than you can really afford. Make sacrifices for it. Have it tuned every few months. Have the action 'regulated' every few years—if you can find that scarce human being, a genuine, properly trained and experienced regulator. Avoid excessive heat, excessive draughts, excessive dampness, and the excessive dryness of central heating.

Love all mankind, but be a snob about pianos.

III

Friend or Foe

(How a piano likes to be used)

When recording was in its infancy and radio was not yet invented it was easy to make a friend of the piano. If nobody played the piano there was liable to be no music. Since life without music is dreary there was always a welcome for the piano-playing member of a family. In my own home people used to bring their music to young Sidney to 'try over'. What with their music and my own I tried over Rubinstein's *Melody in F*, Beethoven's 'Moonlight' Sonata, musical-comedy selections, Chopin's *Funeral March*, Sinding's *The Rustle of Spring*, and a *potpourri* from Gounod's *Faust*. I played the opening prayers of Tchaikovsky's *1812 Overture*, skipped the difficult battle scenes, and clanged the bells of victory at the end.

Even when I left my first teacher and went to a 'real professor' I played not only his sort of music but everyone else's. I played the piano because the weather was bad or because some new piece had captured me. I played because I had been bullied and needed to hit something. I played because Beethoven was grand and Mendelssohn was pretty, and I assured the ghost of Chopin that even a schoolboy could understand romance and tragedy. I played to exercise my muscles, to put off doing my homework (or to celebrate finishing it). I played to show off.

I seldom practised with diligence. If I played something over and over again it was for one of two reasons. Either I was enjoying a second helping of something I enjoyed, *or I was searching for some knack that would make hours of practice unnecessary.*

(Let me see now . . . perhaps if I jab my thumb just there . . . and look at the hardest note two beats before I play it . . . or, jumping to and fro, concentrate on the *fro*. . . .)

If I found the knack I was looking for I played the page again and again in sheer triumph. How clever of me! I had discovered how to play without practising. Or had I really discovered how to practise?

Of course, when I grew up to be a serious student I had to learn practice-methods, which we shall come to later, but as a schoolboy I learned many tricks of the trade, not to mention some bits of low cunning that disguised my failings. The piano was my friend, and its gift to me was a pair of strong hands.

A good friend is sometimes a foe. My piano demanded more scales and arpeggios than I wanted to give. We quarrelled over this, but my piano was right.

And there were pieces of music that at first seemed unfriendly. My favourite approach to most music was to 'play it over'. How could I practise a piece if I didn't know what it was like? But Bach's fugues did not permit this. Other pieces by Bach could sometimes be managed, but I thought 'titchy little minuets' very boring. Even when I was a teenager and could master a Liszt Rhapsody with quite a bit of youthful virtuosity I still couldn't 'see' a Bach fugue. In this respect I was a late developer. When at last I caught on, I went through a phase of fugomania.

Friendship with the piano is not the same for everyone. A child may possess the mysterious something we call a gift for music, but if he is not fairly brainy too he may never manage the great masterpieces. He will either play light music to amuse himself and his friends—which is certainly better than boring them—or he will be one of those earnest strivers who (bless their hearts!) do try to maintain some sort of standard even if they never achieve artistry.

It is only fair to say that a gift plus brains is sometimes devoted to the serious, professional performance of light music. Occasionally I meet a skilled light pianist who is highbrow, imaginative, and devoted to Mozart and Stravinsky. Just occasionally.

IV

Looking at Music

***

One of the chief obstacles to friendship with your piano is the difficulty of reading music. Some people dodge this by playing by ear, and the best ear-players certainly do make friends with the piano. But the man who plays only by ear is usually limited to simple tunes and harmonies and perhaps he is confined to one favourite key.

Playing by ear is immensely important. So is improvising. We shall come to both later, but let us start with reading.

I often think that the best way to learn this would be to find a tune by ear and then write it on paper. Imagine, if you like, that you are wrecked on a desert island and that a crate containing a piano has been washed ashore without damage. (Unlikely, but let's pretend.) Having built a shelter and found food and water you spend your spare time in finding tunes. You then wish to write them. You take a board from the crate and some charcoal from the fire and draw a diagram. The way to do it is shown in Fig. 3. The tune in the picture is exactly what a castaway would sing: 'My Bonnie lies over the Ocean.' The system of lines and spaces is very clear. The vertical strokes—the barlines—come immediately before the regularly accented syllables.

Looking at the picture you may find it a bit of an eye-opener to see music written piano-size and horizontal instead of small and vertical.

It must be admitted that standard notation only roughly fits the keyboard. Our notation pretends that the black key between F and G is a sharpened F or a flattened G whereas it has a perfect right to its own existence without borrowing a name from a neighbour. There is a Dutch

19

FIG. 3

Fig. 3 shows how a stave corresponds with a keyboard. This stave is, so to speak, 'piano size'. The notes on the stave are level with their 'opposite numbers' on the keyboard.

The tune is My Bonnie lies over the Ocean. A vertical line before a note shows where accent normally lies—My BONnie lies Over the Ocean.

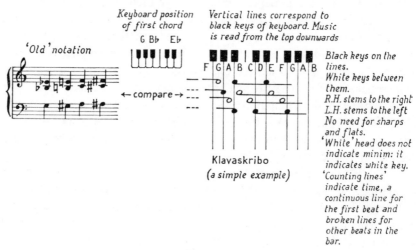

Keyboard position
of first chord

G Bb Eb

'Old' notation

← compare →

Vertical lines correspond to
black keys of keyboard. Music
is read from the top downwards

F G A B C D E F G A B

Black keys on the
lines.
White keys between
them.
R.H. stems to the right
L.H. stems to the left
No need for sharps
and flats.
'White' head does not
indicate minim: it
indicates white key.
'Counting lines'
indicate time, a
continuous line for
the first beat and
broken lines for
other beats in the
bar.

Klavaskribo
(a simple example)

FIG. 3a

system called Klavarskribo in which lines run *down* the page in twos and threes corresponding to the black keys. 'Black notes' are placed on these lines: 'white notes' between them. Sharps and flats simply disappear. There are other clever ideas including counting-lines to help the reading of time. A large library of pieces printed in this way is available, and thousands of Dutch teachers and pupils swear by it. There is a Klavarskribo Institute in London, and the system is spreading in 'emergent countries' where much must be learned as quickly and simply as possible. I wish it had been invented about the time when the piano was taking over from the harpsichord. See Fig. 3a.

Reading normal notation you can borrow the basic idea of counting-lines. This is nobody's patent and has been used—far too seldom—for many years. See Ex. 1.

Ex. 1

People think that the problem of reading is to find the notes. They forget the other problem—to find the moment of sound. It is often true that if you know *when* to play you know *what* to play—as everybody knows who has played in an orchestra under a conductor with a clear beat.

I sometimes beat time with a ruler on the page. The ruler comes down on the note and hides it. This action says *Now!*, and at the same time nudges the pupil's eye to the next beat. His eye cannot linger on the note already struck: I have hidden it. A series of carefully timed and placed taps with a ruler across the page can work wonders. (Teacher must stand on the left of the pupil.)

A piece of sight-reading must be seen by the eye, heard by the ear, and felt by the muscles. Reading a piece away from the keyboard you should be able to hear what is written and feel the piece in your fingers—feeling the keyboard that isn't there.

Always remember there are three meanings to the word *beat*.

1. A beat is a moment in time. You play *on* the beat.

2. A beat is a duration, the time between the tick and tock of the metronome. You play notes *in* or *during* a beat.

3. A beat is beaten. It is accent, stress, emphasis. It is the heart-beat, the pulse that drives the blood of the music. It is march and dance and clapping of hands or the gentle sway of a graceful walk. Nos. 1 and 2 are carefully studied in fear of examiners. No. 3 should be explored for the love of music.

Pay attention to time. Master it but do not let it master you. Time *can* be the enemy of rhythm. Observe printed accents, stress-marks, *sforzandi* etc., but remember that, apart from these, accent is going on all the time in all its variety. The counting-lines in my illustration are written in varying lengths—the longer the louder. For the sake of basic accent, even though you will vary it later—try playing a passage as in Ex. 2.

For some people the whole business of basic time and accent is neatly made clear by saying 'French time-names'. See Ex. 3.

* * *

Good reading at sight is a rare skill. Poor readers excuse themselves by saying they haven't got the gift. It is true that the gifted ones will always do best, but there is no reason why so many should be so bad, expecially since poor reading is the principal reason why most boys and girls abandon piano playing.

There are three cures for weakling readers. One—a nasty medicine that's good for you—is to count beats out loud. This is a marvellous cure for all sorts of failings: mistakes and stumbles are often due to poor timing.

The second cure is to play duets with someone who is just a little better than you are. Get acquainted with, say, Haydn's symphonies in this way. Go on from duet playing to accompanying songs.

The third cure is to buy the popular music of the moment and play that. You know the tune, you know the way it goes rhythmically, but you still have to read in the key provided and you must sort out the accompaniment. You also know when you have made a mistake—which is not always true of reading a dreary sight-reading test.

*   *   *

Combined rhythms often cause trouble. This is a case where actions speak louder than words. Look at Ex. 4. Do what it tells you. This will be better than pages of explanation.

Ex. 4

Practise as written. Then in bar 1 play the G's with the left thumb.
In bar 2 play the G's with the right thumb.

This should lead to :–

V

Phrasing and Pedalling

Give yourself middle C as a starting note and sing 'Twinkle, Twinkle Little Star'. Now make the piano sing *twinkle*, making sure that *twink* is louder than *-le*. Start again. Make the piano sing *twinkle, twinkle* (loud-soft, loud-soft). Continue with *little* (loud-soft) and end with a firm *star*. Take a breath. Make the hand take a breath. This consists of lifting the whole arm and holding it airborne above the keys.

You have now played a bit of music, you have sorted out the accented and unaccented notes, and you have taken a breath that ends one bit of music and takes in air for the next utterance. You have learned the most important lesson you will ever learn about phrasing.

Do not believe the 'rule' that the end of a phrase should be shaded off. The word *star* is on a first-beat and is strong. If, instead of *star*, we sang *planet* we would shade off the ending, the weak syllable, the second beat.

Simple words in simple songs generally keep in step. Words and music illuminate one another. Advanced music is another matter, but

Ex. 5

CHOPIN: Nocturne Op. 9, No. 2

Love must I ne-ver ne-ver hope to see   thee?

'Hope' is the emotional climax with slightly ex- -tended tenuto.
'See' is the metrical climax.
'Thee' is quietened.

Accentuation is suggested by my words.

24

even there I sometimes invent some simple words to convey the under-lying accentuation. See Ex. 5. My words are not good enough for Chopin's music but they are good enough for a teacher giving a piano lesson. Many a piece called 'Romance' or 'Intermezzo' or 'Caprice' or 'Prelude' could be given the title that Mendelssohn invented—'Song without Words'—and they should be played as though they were songs *with* words. Words often make music flexible and lead us towards *rubato*—a subject we must return to.

* * *

Words and music suggest singer and accompanist. In thousands of pieces the treble is the song and the bass is the accompaniment. Play the one louder and the other softer and you have done something supremely important. The situation is not always as simple as this—as we shall find —but every child should learn early in life to play two hands at different strengths. The trick is more easily learned at 7 than at 14 years of age.

* * *

Phrasing and balance of tone seem to draw our attention to pedalling. This should also be learned early. Many difficult knacks come easiest to infants. When it comes to climbing trees, standing on our heads, or learning to swim we grow stupider as we grow older. Learning to manage the pedals on a piano is much easier than learning to manage the pedals on a bicycle.

When I was a little boy and couldn't really reach the pedals I sat on the very edge of the stool—and why not?—got my right heel on the floor and began to experiment. I learned a number of things by myself but I must confess that the really important trick called *legato* pedalling had to be explained by my teacher. I knew the word *legato*. It meant 'joined'. A finger holding a note had to stay down until the very instant when the next note sounded. This joining of sounds produced what was called smooth playing.

I could do this, note after note, in a melody but I could not play chords smoothly. In going from one chord to the next I had to give up the first

Ex. 6

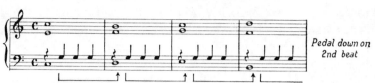

Pedal down on
2nd beat

Two easy examples from Schumann's 'Album for the Young'

Chorale

Little Study

BRAHMS: Intermezzo Op.118, No.1 *An example of complex pedalling*

chord, sort out my fingers in silence, and then play the next chord. What was to be done? My teacher showed me what he called syncopated pedalling—syncopated because the foot stayed down when the arm rose but came up when the arm fell.

If this seems complicated, try a trick away from the piano. Sit with your feet flat on the floor. Smack your right knee and, *at the same instant,* raise the right toes, keeping the heel on the floor. Try this a few times and be sure that the smack *coincides exactly* with the rise of the toes.

Now for the next stage. Repeat what you did before and then, a second later, put the sole of the shoe back on the floor. Now we have:

ARM: Raise & Smack   Raise & Smack
FOOT: Up . . . down   Up . . . down

Since it is natural to stamp on the beat it will seem unnatural to put the pedal down *after* playing the chord. Similarly it will seem unnatural to raise the arm without raising the pedal.

Tricky? Yes, of course. Piano playing is difficult—like playing any other game that you take seriously.

Later stages are shown in Ex. 6. And we shall return to the subject of pedalling—this kind and others—when we discuss beauty of tone. But—I beg of you—conquer basic *legato* pedalling first. It will be hard to begin with, it will suddenly 'come easy', and it will be your friend for life.

VI

The Use of Your Self

Sit with your right side against a table that is the same height from the floor as a piano keyboard. Lay your right hand and arm on the flat surface, resting them easy. Try drumming with the fingers, each in turn, and do not use any muscles except the ones necessary for finger action. Look at the illustrations of hand and finger positions. If your playing physique is undeveloped you will not be able to assume the best 'shape' immediately, but keep it in mind: we shall return to it.

Try tapping the table with your thumb, leaving the other fingers undisturbed. (In pianist's language the thumb is a finger—No. 1.) Do something similar with the 2nd finger (forefinger). Then the 3rd. When you get to the 4th, you will discover that the human hand was not evolved for the purpose of playing the piano. To move the 4th easily you must move the 5th with it. The 5th itself can be independent.

The lift of the finger need not be high. What matters is firmness and precision. If the arm is undisturbed we can describe this as 'pure' finger action.

Now something much harder. Except for the thumb, lift the fingers a quarter-inch off the table. Now make a double movement. At one and the same instant, lift the thumb and put down the 2nd finger. Then, at one and the same instant, lift the 2nd finger and put down the 3rd. And so on. . . . This is difficult. But important. What is also difficult and important is that you should turn your chair right round and try all this with the left hand. Timing is what matters—the up and the down exactly coinciding, producing the *legato* touch I mentioned in the last chapter.

28

Now try a new thumb movement, not up and down but in and out. Teach your thumb to tuck itself under the arch of fingers (see Fig. 4 (a) and (b)). When it comes out again let it remain slightly bent. Train both thumbs.

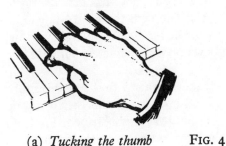

(a) *Tucking the thumb under the fingers*   FIG. 4   (b) *How not to move the thumb under*

FIG. 5 *Awkward hand action hinged at the wrist*

*   *   *

Having discovered something about action and sensation in the fingers, let us make hand movements. Leaving the arm on the table, lift the hand, hinged from the wrist (see Fig. 5). This is an awkward movement unless kept very small. If you make this small movement over and over again quickly you will feel a reaction in the arm. From all this we learn that hand actions are small and seldom 'pure'.

Forearm action, hinged from the elbow, can now be tried. It can be done, but it is awkward. 'Pure' forearm action that leaves the upper arm quite still is not of practical use.

*   *   *

What we use most effectively is the whole arm, whether in small movements or large. Lift the whole arm, keeping the forearm level, parallel with the table-top. Bring it down so that finger-tips and elbow arrive on the table-top together. Try varying altitudes and varying speeds of ascent and descent. Now move the arm to the right but not in an arc. That is to say: move the elbow out to the right in line with the hand. As you go further, help the action by leaning your body. There are limits to this, but in general we try to keep the elbow opposite the notes, not held into the side of the body.

Turn round and make left-and-out movements with the other arm.

Now, instead of sliding from a near position to a far one, try flying up and over. This action, in practice, is not always arch-shaped. Fly from the near position to a position in the air directly above the far position and complete your flight by a straight-down descent. Think of a converse action for the return journey.

Practise this with the other arm.

Perhaps by now you have become aware that your arms have weight. Hoist this weight into the air and then let it fall like a ton of bricks. Don't drive it down but let it fall 'crash-bang-wallop'. Learn what a truly free fall is though you will seldom use it. We 'fall' in a controlled way in piano playing, and this sort of 'fall' is not truly a *fall*.

Some teachers always talk in terms of weight. They tell their pupils to release varying amounts of weight. This undoubtedly makes people sense their way down to the keys and often produces well-controlled tone. On the other hand it carries the danger of sluggishness. Thinking perpetually of weight, you cannot dart about. I 'teach weight' on occasion, but I am more inclined to talk of athletic descent, at varying speeds, towards the tone-target. There are only limited opportunities of leaning on the piano.

In any kind of touch your wrist must be firm yet springy, transmitting the arm's thoughts to the fingers. It must be free to move or to stay still, never fidgeting, and it must never flabbily flop.

Let us now leave the table and apply our actions to the piano keys. On the table I began with fingers and proceeded to the whole arm. On the keyboard let us begin with the arm and proceed to the fingers.

Lift the arm, horizontal from elbow to finger-tips, above the keys, say 6 inches above. Stay there and pretend that your arm is lying on an imaginary table. This fanciful notion should help you to stay up with minimum effort. Now try coming down to the keys from different heights and at different speeds. If you like, do this with a clenched fist. Go down unhesitatingly, through the 'surface of the keys' to the key-bed position.

Unclench your fist and play notes. Coming down rather fast you will discover that your fingers need a certain degree of grip if they are not to collapse on landing. The degree of grip varies with loudness, and your sensation of grip depends on how muscular your hand is. Good fingers are neither steel nor rubber. They are muscle . . . and they have the sense of touch.

A pianist needs the listening finger. Also a thinking wrist.

It needs confidence to go straight into the keys without hesitating, without making sure at surface level. Cultivate this confidence if you can, and then your arms will, so to speak, conduct the music. This is better than rushing ahead, slowing down at key-surface and then waiting for the music to catch up.

Skilled and confident pianists, so far from hesitating on the way down, actually accelerate, just as a games player accelerates the movement of bat or racket as he nears the ball, or as a footballer accelerates his leg towards the football. This general principle applies even to gentle actions. Just watch a fine player of billiards or snooker gently performing a really delicate shot. The action may be small and slow but it accelerates.

I am not saying that the key-surface must never be felt first and pushed later. But it is one thing to do this deliberately and sensitively: it is another to get somewhere near a new note as early as possible, anxiously, afraid of mistakes.

In this connection, do not use rests as a mere opportunity to get somewhere. A long rest may be a stillness, a period of reflection or doubt. It has to be part of the performance. If you fidget near the next note, well in advance of due time, you will be like a singer who takes a breath and then doesn't sing.

Stillness is important, but music is mostly movement. For this reason I often compare piano playing to tennis rather than golf. It is true that a key stays still like a golf ball awaiting your strike, but the note in the music doesn't. The note presents itself at a certain moment in time, and it must be converted into sound there and then.

31

I am no great games player but I feel a kinship with tennis champions. Perhaps I ought to feel more kinship with ballet dancers, for there is a powerful and important element of gesture, mime, and acting in piano playing. Efficiency by itself produces a cold performance.

*   *   *

Still postponing consideration of the fingers, fold your arms. Now lean quickly and heavily on the keyboard, striking umpteen notes at once. Try this not only in mid-keyboard but at the top and bottom ends. Accept the idea that body action can lend strength to a chord, can take the arms to where they have to go, and can, in certain circumstances, 'embrace' a phrase with intensity. Now play some chords and include some degree of 'body-ness' in your action. Avoid mere crouching over the keyboard. Avoid behaving like a piano remover.

As you discover more and more bits of your 'playing-self', remember that treble and bass are seldom symmetrical. Look at Ex. 7 and consider which does what.

Ex. 7

R.H. swung over L.H. "placed" until just before final note.

In music that seems to demand a two-arm swing you may find it best to swing one arm boldly while carefully placing the other (see Ex. 7b).

Use your eyes on the keyboard where necessary. A great deal of athletic skill is hindered by the constant cry of 'Look at the music'.

I must not exaggerate the elements of aim and flight. Admittedly a good deal of piano playing consists of going to a key at just the right moment and 'giving it a little push'. But even this little push is a miniature version of the plunge down. It must never be a nervous shilly-shallying poke.

VII

More About Fingers

Finger action is highly unnatural. There is nothing like it in games-playing. Somehow we must make this artificial activity 'second nature'.

Let us go back to hand-shape. Crush a handkerchief into a ball. Start to unclench till you get to the point where the handkerchief is in danger of falling to the floor. With my hand and a man-size handkerchief I can use this demonstration to produce a good hand-shape. Can you divine what I mean? Some people find hand-shape by clasping their knee cap. Anyway the ideal shape can be described as half way between stretched out and clenched tight.

On the keyboard many a beginner finds pure finger action impossible. A very young child always pushes his finger from the arm and at first must be allowed to. As time goes on and he plays faster and louder, he will, if touch is neglected, play everything with a 'joggy' action. Even the semiquavers will consist of a succession of little poking actions by the arm and hand.

This is bad. Quite early in the game, this young child must learn to play from a still or a smoothly gliding arm and hand. At first these notes will have to be very soft. Never mind. It remains generally true in piano playing that the quick runs you play with pure finger action should be lighter in tone than long notes and big chords. There is great merit in being able to play a quiet, smooth, even-toned five-finger exercise. Two things to watch:

   1. Each note should be released *exactly* when the next begins.

C

2. The arm should be still, but in a quietly easy way, not rigid.

Gaining strength of finger is a long-term affair. Agility and ease are more important than sheer power in the early years so long as the search for refinement is not exaggerated.

Going on to scales and arpeggios we must combine the true finger action with the gliding arm. Remember to move the upper arm away from the body as you travel outwards. Cultivate a true thumb-under action. There are too many young pianists who have four active fingers plus a lazy thumb that has to be hoisted about with the help of the elbow.

If you play exercises in different keys, learn to play among the black keys (see Fig. 6). There are times when white keys are not in front of

FIG. 6 *First finger lying between black keys*

black keys but between them. Start with the thumb on E flat and notice how the fingers for F and G lie alongside or between black keys. In a good many scales and arpeggios the arms must travel not only along the keyboard but across it.

Talking of exercises, these may be described as piano playing apart from music. Most books of exercises are too full of every problem in every way in every key, but selected exercises intelligently done can be fascinating and rewarding.

However, if you want athletic skill, you will find no better friends than scales and arpeggios. You need variety of rhythm, variety of *legato* and *staccato* touch, and variety of tone. Look at my page of examples (Ex. 8) and see if you too cannot be a composer of scales and arpeggios.

Ex. 8

C major~ in lengthening pieces

continue to add an extra beat up to
4 octaves.
Repeat process in downward direction.

D major arpeggio with strong accents

etc.

Eb major ~ a pair of notes and an echo. Observe fingering.

E minor ~ in 10ᵗʰ

For more advanced players:
minor double thirds

At each rest half-clench the
hand, relaxing the fingers

etc.

Play truly on the finger-tips, not on the underside of the finger nor right over on the nail. And keep your finger-nails very short. (I am sorry, girls, but you must.)

Playing an arpeggio do not try to find too many notes in advance. If you are playing a broken chord, C E G and top C, there is no need to have your 5th finger stretched out ready for the top note before you have even played the bottom one (see Fig. 7). Nor should you leave the thumb over the bottom C once the note is finished. Put it this way: when you play bottom C your 5th finger should be somewhere near A; when you play top C your thumb should be relaxed somewhere near F.

FIG. 7 *There is no need to measure out all the notes of a broken chord in advance*

Think seriously about finger relaxation. So many people seem to know only about arm relaxation. In fact, let us now embark on the subject of relaxation in general.

VIII

Relaxation

When you first discover the importance of relaxation you can easily be so excited as to think that it is the answer to all problems. Relax! Loosen up! Avoid tension!

Beware! You cannot play with vigour and precision if your fingers are like the plumage of a feather-duster. You cannot play if you sit on the stool with an air of weariness and exhaustion.

I suppose a person is truly relaxed if he has swooned away in a dead faint. What you and I have to do is to make bits and pieces of ourselves faint and revive at exactly the right moment. Can you activate one finger and relax four? Can you play fortissimo with one arm and leave the other lying easily on your lap? Do you know whether you are relaxing fingers, hand, or arm?

Think of strap-hanging in an underground train. The train stops. You can relax your arm *above your head* so long as your fingers continue to grip: the arm is slung between strap and shoulder. Or you can relax your fingers *above your head* so long as the arm holds itself up: your fingers are now resting in the strap. Or you can relax arm and fingers, in which case the arm will fall to your side. This is a simple exercise in becoming aware of areas of relaxation.

Now hold a simple chord. If you want to rest your arm you must hold on with finger-grip. If you want to reduce fatigue of the fingers you must make your arm support itself.

Another experiment. Arm in the air, distinguish between relaxed fingers dangling from the knuckles and (something quite different) a

37

relaxed hand dangling from the wrist (see Fig. 8 (a) and (b)). In my own playing, most of the time I do not dangle the hand. I relax my fingers in the air, reserving the swooning hand for a certain kind of slow and romantic music.

(a) *Relaxed fingers*   Fig. 8   (b) *Relaxed hand*

In slow octaves I relax my fingers between one octave and the next, and I do so as much as possible in fast octaves, 'shaking them out of my sleeve' (as Liszt said).

Back on the keyboard I know that I can sometimes avoid finger fatigue by calling upon the twisting muscles of the arm—say in a rapid alternation between thumb and little finger—but I must always consider which way produces the better effect and I will take the hard way if I prefer the sound. We often have to know two ways of doing one thing. Do the twist. Do it very well. When suitable. Try two kinds of trill, one helped by a to and fro twist of the arm, and the other produced by two fingers doing the work by themselves. The second kind is sometimes (not always) helped by using a scratching action.

Consider body attitudes. Obviously the waist can be considered as a hinge and we can move from an upright position to a crouching one. But sometimes we should move the *waist* itself nearer the keys, almost as though beginning to get out of the chair. A slight movement of this kind often goes together with a moment of intensity and is followed by—you might say—a slight withdrawal of the stomach.

Consider your feet. Many people press a pedal far too hard and then release it with an audible bump. On a well adjusted piano I never push the pedal as far as it will go and I never take my foot right off the pedal. Some pianists keep both feet on the pedals all the time. For my part I tuck my left foot under the stool unless the piece has a great deal of *una corda*: I feel more athletic in that attitude. My right foot is always on the pedal, whether I use it or not. Feet flat on the floor look very goody-goody and anxious.

When experimenting with action and relaxation, do not be afraid of exaggeration at first. You never know *how* much movement to make until you have tried *too* much. No doubt there is an art that conceals art, but be sure you have something to conceal.

Minimize effort, but be willing to use great effort where necessary. And avoid gestures of anxiety like nodding at accents, screwing up your eyes, pouting your lips, hunching your shoulders, holding your breath, and grunting.

From time to time take a look at yourself. Review the height of your piano stool. As you grow taller cut it down, taking a saw to the legs if necessary. Sitting high may make you feel strong, but sitting low encourages delicacy. Be strong enough to sit reasonably low.

IX

The Beauty-of-Tone Problem

***

$\mathbf{P}$ush down any key on the piano and you will hear the tone built in by the maker. You can play it louder or softer, you can hold the note for a longer or shorter time, but you cannot make it more beautiful than it is. I can say, a little illogically, that you can make it ugly if you slap it flat-fingered, introducing noise as you strike the surface, or if you bang it beyond what the designer intended. Even then you will find that an ugly bang in the treble becomes less disagreeable if a chord is substituted for a single note . . . perhaps because your force is shared among several notes.

On a 'cello, a clarinet, and many other instruments, a single note is music. Not so on a piano. Magic begins with a succession of notes. Nobody can be a great pianist on one note.

We have already discovered that playing becomes more beautiful as we make true contrast between 'song' and accompaniment and becomes even more so if we reveal strands of song *in* accompaniment. Remarkably few people can play one hand more gently than the other, and still fewer can make one note stand out from a chord. How to do this is shown in Ex. 9.

Ex. 9

Then play these chords, making a line of the inside notes.

Then there is this mysterious something called *cantabile*—'singing tone'. Some teachers argue that you can increase the fullness and round-ness and depth and quality of a note without making it louder. My view is that you can appear to do so, but singing notes *are* louder than accom-paniment (or accompaniment is softer than singing notes) and *cantabile* tone is never literally pianissimo.

The problem solves itself in many pieces if we make long notes *loud enough to last their length.* Take Beethoven's 'Moonlight' Sonata—the first movement. Look at Ex. 10 and think of the time as 12 quavers in a bar. It is true that Beethoven's time signature means two minims, but for our present purpose think of 12 beats. In that case a dotted minim must be heard for the whole length of 9 beats. Is *your* dotted minim audible for as long as that? If not, is it your fault or have you an inadequate piano? Anyway, to obey Beethoven's demand for 9 beats of sound, we must dis-obey his *pianissimo.* It is this sort of creative disobedience—really a more penetrating obedience—that is a large part of what we call interpretation. Ask yourself how loudly dare you play the melody without giving a *forte* effect, and how softly can you play the accompaniment without throwing away all its interest and beauty. The bass notes must have length too.

Ex.10

Most pianists find that melody notes can best be projected by arm touch. If you try to use finger touch you have to worry about stronger and weaker fingers. If you use arm touch you need only worry about stronger and weaker pressures channelled through fingers that know how to accept and convey these pressures. The fingers have a job to do, of course, but it is only if the melody contains groups of little notes or ornaments that the fingers spring into active life of their own.

Your arm pushes the key, thinking of the tone that is needed for the duration of the note. But immediately after the note has begun to sound, the arm can half-release the pressure for the remainder of the time. A loud note can be held on with a soft pressure. There are different schools of thought about this. Some people press down on the finger-tips in a way that causes knuckles and the wrist to rise. Following this nudge, the half-release is produced by a falling wrist. For my part, I prefer a downward movement of the whole arm followed by a slight rise. Imagine that your arm is lying along the padded arm of an armchair. Imagine yourself pressing the whole arm down into the sprung padding and then allowing the springs to push the arm up again. Bring this imagined situation to the keyboard and pretend that the key-bed is upholstered and extends all the way to your elbow. Push down half an inch deep and come up a quarter.

This kind of playing produces a sort of undulation from note to note. Experiment with varying degrees of this, and do not be afraid of it. Sometimes the half-release turns into complete release. The pedal takes charge of *legato* (and why not?) and the arm is airborne before the next note. As far as the hinges of the arm and hand are concerned, share the action between the wrist and the big knuckles. In Fig. 9 you will see how one hand can teach the other the sensation of knuckle undulation. As for the wrist, avoid arching it up too high or letting it sag right down.

FIG. 9 *Left hand helping right hand knuckles to rise and fall*

The longer notes of a melody should be pushed 'deeper into the upholstery'. Let us say, by way of general guidance, that minims and crotchets are deep. Quavers are shallower—played with a succession of smaller arm movements or else played by fingers under a smoothing-out pressure that travels along the keyboard through the group. Semiquavers are finger notes with perhaps slight arm pressure applied to a note *on* the beat.

This is only general advice. An infinite variety of pressures goes into artistic *cantabile* touch. As for the accompaniment, this too must be upholstered with judgment. And always remember in romantic music: the 'worse' the discord, the louder you play it. The clash of F against F sharp, for instance, invites accent (see Ex. 11).

Ex.11

Pressure is not always applied straight down. In vigorous accent we often press slightly forward. Gentle accent (not so gentle, please, as to be unheard) may be done with a slight tug, as though drawing and pulling the tone out of the piano. Sometimes we use a sliding contact. Putting the finger-tip at the back end of a key we make a slow pulling, sliding action that starts the sound, continues the sound, and releases the sound. This produces a soft effect without your having to give a gingerly push down or a nervous pull up. Pressure and release are 'meltingly' applied during the pull. It all seems easy yet sure. (See Ex. 12.)

Ex.12

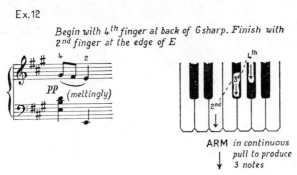

For sensitive approach to tone we have another useful process in which the wrist rotates in a way that describes a circle. Imagine that a small hoop or bangle is held round your wrist but without contact. Now, with your finger on a note, move your wrist to the right, so that it touches the hoop, and then start sliding round and round the inside of the hoop, clockwise or anti-clockwise. This will not make your note sound better, but it may make the *next* note sound better. Properly timed, and slowly swung, this action provides a sensitive approach to the next note, into which you sink as though into a warm bath. I say again: this action *precedes* a note. If the notes are medium-spaced crotchets you can set up a round and round action that plays note after note; but if you produce a long note like this you should then stay still until it is time to approach the next. With a 4-beat note I would stay still for 3 beats and start the circling approach on the 4th.

As in the case of a sliding touch we get a *legatissimo* touch. That is to say, the end of one note merges into the beginning of the next. The effect is rather like tiptoeing across the floor as distinct from ordinary walking.

*　　　*　　　*

Our conjuring tricks with beauty-of-tone depend a great deal on pedalling. We already know basic *legato* pedalling. Now let us learn half-pedalling. With the pedal down, play a loud *staccato* bass octave. If you now move your pedal up and down very quickly you will find you have not quite damped that octave. This failure of the damping mechanism can be put to advantage. See Ex. 13, where the quick half-pedal damps the high notes but leaves a residue of tied-over sound in the bass.

Ex.13

Then there is half-damping. The pedal is half-down, half-up, sensitively oscillating between the levels for sutaining and damping. This is used for brilliant passages that would sound dry without pedal and smudged with it. The pedal produces a kind of half-way tremble that gives glitter without smudge.

Sometimes, playing detached chords, we put the foot down with the chord and pick it up with the rest. This 'direct pedalling' does not affect the duration, it does not sustain the chord; but by taking all the dampers off the strings it conjures up some extra sympathetic vibration and adds to the 'ring' of the sound.

Should pedal be used across a rest? The answer is that in music composed before the pedal was invented—that is to say before Beethoven—a rest is a silence. In music of the romantic era this is not always true. Instead of saying 'silent *now*', the rest seems to say 'begin a fade-away hereabouts'. Though the foot stays down, the rise of the arm into the air seems, in some mysterious way, to introduce a breath before a new phrase—especially if *rubato* rhythm has produced a slight slowing down at the end of the phrase.

* * *

Rubato (the word means 'robbed') is the strangest kind of stealing. It is true that some notes may be robbed of their true length, causing the music to hurry, but others are given more than their due. This conjuring trick with beauty, this flexible beat, seldom works well if an individual note is suddenly lengthened or shortened. And the whole thing is a failure if there is so much distortion of rhythm as to make people think they are hearing three beats where only two are written. It is most suitable in music that resembles love-songs, and it consists of cunning and slight increases and lessenings of speed. If I play *rubato* rhythm properly you should be able to write a phrase you have just heard me play and still get the time-values correct. I may linger slightly on a specially heartfelt note, I may slightly exaggerate the sigh of a small rest, I may hurry towards an anguished discord but, if you are a musician, you will still know what the time values are. If I play a good *rubato* in a concerto I will not irritate the conductor or flummox the orchestra.

A hastening or a slowing down should generally be too slight to allow anyone to mark *accelerando* or *rallentando* in the copy, and, in any case, these changes of speed should not be completely calculated. They must seem to be done on the spur of the moment. Nevertheless, cunning and calculation do enter into *rubato* playing, and it is nearly always advisable when slowing down at the last note of a phrase to continue slowly through any accompanying notes that belong to that last note.

Unfortunately, *rubato* playing cannot be completely described on paper: it has to be imparted by example. When you first attempt it you may find yourself going along by fits and starts, but Ex. 14 may be helpful as a suggestion.

Ex.14   RUBATO (a suggestion)

CHOPIN: Etude in E, Op. 10, No 3. *with slight and subtle accel. and rit.*

Rubato varies in degree from composer to composer. A *rubato* suitable for a Chopin Nocturne will be disastrous for a Bach Minuet. Nevertheless, do not believe that a minuet, being ballroom music, must go in strict time. It must persuade dancers to move elegantly, and it must be animated by a living pulse, not nudged along by the tick of clockwork. There is very little music that has no *rubato* whatsoever. Even a well disciplined march is not designed for wooden soldiers (unless the title says so).

There is no better training in *rubato* than to accompany a good singer.

*   *   *

Romantic beauty is all very well, but music must not be indiscriminately beautified. A nocturne may be played in a sweetly romantic fashion,

46

but the character of a battle piece can be ruined by 'beauty treatment'. I have known people who are so afraid of bad tone that they never play a true *fortissimo*.

If a piece has a descriptive title behave accordingly. You would not smile through a funeral march: why frown through a Gigue by Bach— even if the technical difficulties are serious? You would not dance stiffly: why sit stock still while playing a waltz.

Think of what you look like: have the right air about you. Know how to be charming in a Mozart Minuet, virile when Beethoven says *con brio*, gipsy-ish in a Liszt Rhapsody, reflective in a Bach Chorale. A *forte* may mean strong and calm in one piece, desperate and frenzied in another. Know how to play as though grinding your teeth—or as though pronouncing a blessing.

Do not nod at accents as though you were elderly and anxious, do not bow up and down as though worshipping an idol, but do know how to move about the piano. Distinguish between accents that persuade and accents that compel. Make a list of adjectives, and see which of them apply to the piece you are playing. For instance: light, dark, old, young, masculine, feminine, confident, hesitant, posh, vulgar, sophisticated, spiritual, commanding, coquettish, sexy, puritan, amusing, tragic. Can you apply these words to your own playing? Can your friends guess which adjective you have in mind as you play?

Another way of bringing a performance to life is to think of the orchestra. Though much music is purely pianistic, we often play passages that have a trumpety sound or a woody thinness or a string tone or a clang of percussion. 'Think brass'—you need not decide whether you mean horn or trombone. If your sonata were a symphony where would *you* put cymbals in the score?

If you like, imagine yourself as conductor. Having decided what you would tell the players, tell yourself.

There are silky pieces and craggy pieces, town pieces and country pieces, educated pieces and simple pieces, godly pieces and devil's pieces.

*   *   *

Very seldom do we literally 'obey the expression'. Many a *crescendo* has its moment of reduced sound: many a *diminuendo* is not a gradual decrease but a succession of reductions phrase by phrase, not note by note. A softness may be a whisper in the ear or, quite different, a shout from far away. And there is all the difference in the world between the *forte* that says 'I love thee' and the *forte* that says 'I'll kill you'.

X

The Design Problem

There are some kinds of music in which romantic adjectives seem out of place. A simple two-part Invention is what it says it is—an invention. The top part does *this*: the bottom part does *that*. Look! Listen! Isn't it interesting the way the notes go!

When we come to fugues, they are seldom such 'pure music' as they may seem on the surface. There are all sorts of feelings behind the intricate pattern. But we do have to begin by making the pattern clear so that the listener can hear what each 'part' or 'voice' is doing. At a particular moment, one voice may need to stand clear of the others. This may be difficult if three or four voices are moving along together, so we usually approach the problem through simpler music that Bach wrote for his own family.

Let us begin with a simple two-part Invention—the one in F, No. 8. My Ex. 15 may suggest a way of 'seeing' the music and sorting out the parts. My *ff* and *pp* are, of course, tremendous exaggerations, but due proportion often comes from exaggerations gradually reduced.

It is no use studying one Invention. You cannot play one properly until you have practised half a dozen.

Unfortunately for us, Bach wrote most of his music without marks of speed or force. His colleagues and pupils were accustomed to his ways and knew how to play the music. When the piano replaced earlier instruments like the harpsichord and clavichord, and particularly when romantic composers went in for dramatic expressiveness, heart-on-sleeve, Bach's music was published with all sorts of additions put there

Ex.15

BACH: Two-part Invention in F

The high voice up to here, ... *the high voice up to here,*

the low voice up to here, ... *the low voice up to here.*

by editors and other so-called authorities. Many of the slurs and fortes and crescendoes we see in our copies are false and foolish, but few students can cope with a text that has no instructions at all. If you are taking piano lessons I hope your teacher knows good editions from bad.

There are two important problems to solve in a fugue. One is 'how long is a bit of Bach'; the other is—which voice should we particularly listen to at a given moment?

The 'bit of Bach' problem can often be solved by asking yourself: 'If I had several keyboards, as on an organ, when would I jump from one keyboard to another—where does one thing end and another begin?'

The other problem was solved for me by my teacher. He would select a suitable section and then ask me to play it first with the top voice loudest; then with the middle voice loudest; and finally with the bottom voice loudest.

When I could bring out any voice at will, he said 'Well, Sidney, I won't say you can now play fugues, but I will say you are entitled to have a go.'

How did I conquer this difficulty? What I did was to play the notes of one voice firmly while pretending to play the other notes (touching each key but not pressing it down). This was extremely difficult, but it worked. I really did learn part-playing. Try it. It is very hard, but you may learn to play counterpoint triumphantly for the rest of your life. Once it comes easy, it is easy.

In learning to disentangle parts in a fugue you will probably go through a phase of bringing out the 'subject' of the fugue wherever it reappears. You may overdo it. You may then meet someone who will argue that these 'entries' are all the same theme: it is the other parts that are interesting. The fact is, however, that a clear entry of the subject is often an exciting moment and in many cases should be 'sung' prominently and right through to its end. But the other parts are not to be 'chucked away'. To get a fugue into proportion calls for intelligence, insight, and experience. You must cultivate all three.

From fugue playing you will learn a great many subtleties of touch and may be surprised to discover how these help you to play romantic music. Never forget that Chopin was a passionate admirer of Bach's fugues. I would go so far as to say that if you cannot play fugues you cannot play a Chopin Ballade.

XI

How to Practise

I once asked an infant prodigy 'How much do you practise?' Young and innocent, he said, 'As much as I need.' The perfect answer! Perhaps he knew what I know, that *the object of practice is not to practise.*

The object of practice is to find out how a thing is done . . . so that it is *done*. I am not talking about all the qualities of fine playing: I am talking of technical certainty and confidence.

The first process is to discover the best and most effective fingering—not necessarily the fingering in the copy. Old-fashioned editors were far too fond of changing fingers on a repeated note and they went to absurd lengths to avoid thumb on a black key. Good fingering is often unorthodox. Find it. Fix it. Your muscles must know for certain whose turn comes next.

Take your eyes off the page and consider your actions. Look at them. See inside yourself. Don't just get to the next note: time yourself on to it so that your rhythm of action corresponds with the rhythm of the piece. Too often I have to say to a young pianist, 'Your notes are in time but *you* aren't.' Behave like the diver who, once he is off the springboard, is committed to make the destined plunge and cannot hesitate or re-think. Dance to the music. Find a flow of action. Travel through the music. Distinguish between the stillness of a stop and the stillness of a hover.

* * *

What many people want to know is how to practise to 'get more technique'. I have set out several practice-methods in Ex. 16. If you try them

Ex.16

BEETHOVEN: Last movement of "Moonlight" Sonata Op.27, No.2.

Practise in ever increasing lengths.

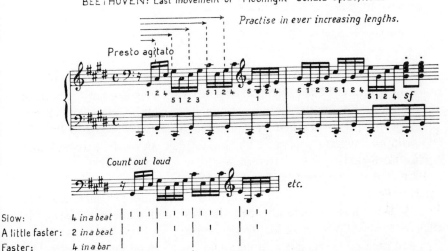

Count out loud

etc.

Slow:	4 in a beat				
A little faster:	2 in a beat				
Faster:	4 in a bar				
Presto:	2 in a bar				

Stop on each beat note

etc.

Drop on each note

etc.

Try dotted rhythms

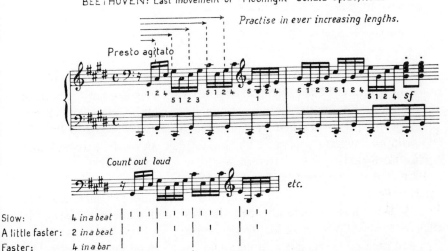
etc.

Do not neglect what the other hand has to play. The easier part needs its share of practice.

all on a difficult passage you will soon discover the one that seems to be most fruitful for that particular example. Take these processes seriously. They save time in the long run.

*   *   *

I know of one successful teacher who insists that every note should be sung, in whatever octave is convenient for your voice—every note from top to bottom, no matter how bad your voice may be. He says that too many people play with their eyes, as though deaf. I would add this: in practising a concerto you must be able to play your own part and sing orchestral melodies at the same time.

I know of another teacher who puts his fist on the pupil's knuckles. The knuckles must be pressed up against his downward pressure, and the fingers are almost pushed through the keyboard while the passage is played slowly. Then he suddenly releases the pressure and says 'Let it fly', and the pupil feels like a runner who has changed out of Wellington boots into canvas shoes.

Not all of these dodges are suitable for beginners. For them nothing is more important than beating time. Without timing there is no co-ordination, no technique.

Remember that a technical problem may have more than one solution. In this connection look at Ex. 17.

*   *   *

If you are playing a group of notes over and over again do not rush from the last note back to the first. Play . . . relax and think . . . play . . . relax and think. The moments of silence are not a waste of time.

Learn to practise in your head, to practise in imagination while you sit in a railway train, but know when to stop.

*   *   *

Many people find a special difficulty in playing ornaments. For example, how do you play a trill? It can *brrr* like an electric bell or be a fast

Ex. 17

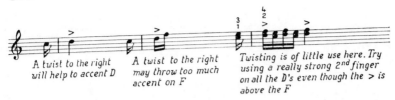

| A twist to the right will help to accent D | A twist to the right may throw too much accent on F | Twisting is of little use here. Try using a really strong 2nd finger on all the D's even though the > is above the F |

Try concentrating attention on
D C D C D (3 2 3 2 3)

CHOPIN: Etude "The Black Key Study"

R and L indicate direction of possible arm twist ~ a side to side vibration when played fast. You must learn to do this. You must also be able to play these notes from an almost still hand using finger technique. Then decide which gives the result you want.

tickatick. I never enjoy the very slow *doodle-doodle* favoured by some Bach players. No doubt a Bach trill is a slower vibration than a Liszt trill, but every trill should *trrrrrill*: an ornament should glitter. See Ex. 18 for a strengthening process.

Ex. 18

Obey the fingering. Invent something similar the other way up and in another key.

A trill often feels easier if you move the hand to and fro across the keyboard—walking back and forth from the lid of the keyboard to the key-edge.

Trills and ornaments are seldom played *forte*. Lightly played they can seem *forte* if you accent the first and last notes.

If an ornament is extremely complex and cannot be crammed into the available time, make a slight *rallentando* before it to avoid a headling rush and a stumble.

*   *   *

Practise to play very well. Do not be a perfectionist. Perfection is for the gods, and they will punish you with a nervous breakdown if you try to be perfect.

XII

Playing With All You've Got

Playing by ear is often regarded as low, common, and vulgar, suitable for community singing in a pub. Yet what kind of musician are you if you can *not* play by ear—cannot play the National Anthem because you have never studied it?

Who plays by ear almost as a way of life? There is the old-fashioned jazz player playing music that has never been seen. There are certain show-business entertainers with a limited but lucrative expertise. There is George—never 'ad a lesson in 'is life. And there is the light composer with a talent for inventing catchy tunes who, aided by a staff of orchestrators, makes a handsome living out of musicals.

All these people have two things in common: they play for pleasure and they are quite unteachable.

In contrast there are many serious pianists who never, alas, play for pleasure. They are teachable but not worth teaching.

As a child I was lucky. Certainly I played by ear (and still do) but I played by sight and by heart as well. My musically ignorant parents saw no reason to forbid playing by ear and I played many a tune against a vamp bass. A few standard chords accompanied most tunes—but not always. One day I tried the 'Soldiers' Chorus' from *Faust* (I heard it first, believe it or not, in a pantomime, *Puss in Boots*) and came to a stop in bar 4. How was that to be harmonized? (See Ex. 19.) I tried every note between middle-C and the C below. B sounded good. B flat didn't. I went on and on and decided that A flat and E were good notes, not know-

57

Ex. 19

The solution for bar 4 was

ing that the A flat should have been called G sharp. Soon I had invented a satisfactory bass and never knew till several years later that it was called (how dreary!) the major triad on the mediant. But long before I was taught harmony I had learned tonic sol-fa. I sang *doh ray me* without knowing that *me* was the mediant. I mentally changed *me* into *doh* and then sang *doh me soh* without knowing that the result was a major triad.

Before long, I was 'making pieces up as I went along' and later developed the useful ability to imitate the way different pianists played in public. And today I have quite a repertoire of pieces I have never seen in my life and can play them in any key you like. What I play by ear I never forget.

BY SIGHT

You play at sight through being inquisitive. 'What's the next piece like?' 'Let's try the symphony four-handed (*you* count and I'll manage the pedal)'. 'Would you like me to play your accompaniment?'

A good sight reader may not be a great artist but he is quite certainly a good musician. But every skill carries with it a corresponding danger. Just as players by ear can be unwilling to read, so can sight readers be unwilling to practise. The good reader can become everyone's helper and dogsbody, never practising his own pieces properly.

Nevertheless you must read. Why? Because there are 48 Bach Fugues, 32 Beethoven Sonatas, 27 Chopin Etudes. . . . Need I say more? And piano music is not the only music.

As for ways of improving your reading, I have dealt with some of these in Chapter IV and will only add that people who peer and stare at the page are never good readers. They are like children who point to each word while reading a story. Reading is a series of glances. No doubt in reading you look at the page and play by feel; but in a duet it is quite possible to glance away from the page at your hands, at your friend's hands, at his page. No good reader has his eyes glued to the music.

BY HEART AND WITH HEART

Some people play from memory naturally. Practising, they look at the music less and less. If you are not gifted in this way, begin by memorizing something short and simple. A short and simple piece can be very impressive if played beautifully. Memorize Schumann's *Träumerei*, not his Concerto.

A few people have photographic memory. They are reading the music in their mind's eye even when the book is shut. A few others, playing by heart, are really playing by ear, remembering the sound of what they learned. Most of us rely heavily on remembering an activity—as dancers do. We have a kind of automatic memory and say to our hands, 'You know what to do: get on with it.'

I belong mainly to the third category, but there is a strong admixture of ear-playing, plus a photograph, not of the patterns on the page, but the patterns on the keys. My eyes say to my hands, '*We* know where you're going.'

If a piece is beginning to be familiar put the music, open, on a low table beside you. Play from memory until the point where memory fails. Look around and down at the page but *do not play at that moment*. Think, remember, look back at your hands, and then resume.

When you can play the piece to yourself, play it to a friend until his presence no longer disturbs you—as it will at first. Then play it to other people on some occasion that is not important. Play to different people on different pianos in private. Then play for an exam or at a competition festival or in a concert.

Why do we bother to memorize when, in fact, we are more afraid of forgetting than of stumbling? The answer is that a truly superb performance is nearly always a memorized one—allowing for the few exceptions.

It is a great mistake to think that you can shut out the audience and concentrate on playing. You must concentrate on playing to the audience —like that great pianist who counted the audience and calculated his percentage of the takings while playing the slow movement. Is this a shocking story? There is a useful truth in it. If someone comes into your music room while you are practising and says you are wanted on the telephone, can you, while continuing to play, say, 'Get his number and tell him I'll ring back presently'?

If you have a deep-seated fear of memorizing, ask a musical friend to dictate a piece you have never seen. Do not look at the music at all. Let your friend play the first phrase. Repeat it yourself, taking it from his hands and through your ears. And so on. Presently you will know a piece that you *must* play from memory because it is the only way you know. And you will remember as surely as a blind man remembers.

I have said that you must play to and for an audience. If, however, you play only to please an audience you will be a mere entertainer. You must also play to please your reasonably critical self and, above all, to please the ghost of the composer. He must haunt you, and you must welcome him.

Think seriously about behaviour and presentation. Know when to be formal; how to bow; when to take an encore. If you are announcing a title, don't (like a 'cellist I know) say 'Saint-Saëns's *Cygne*' or even 'Saint-Saëns's *Swan*'. Say *Ladies and Gentlemen* (they will stop talking) *I should like to play* (they will begin to listen) *a piece called* (there will be an attentive hush) *The Swan* . . . by . . . (they are waiting for it) Saint-Saëns.

Behaviour affects performance. For my part I may rehearse in shirtsleeves, but I put on my jacket and comb my hair before a performance, even in a broadcasting studio.

Hands on my knees, I have a quick think and then I begin. I have no patience with pianists who look up and look down and paw the keys half a dozen times before summoning up courage to play the first note.

I sometimes wish it were possible to say in scientific language that x notes at y velocity need so many units of physical and emotional effort per second. The nearer you can get to this, the more professional you are

. . . provided you avoid the danger of becoming a human tape-recorder endlessly repeating your standard performance.

As for nerves, make up your mind that nerves are part of the game. If you are giving the first performance of a new and difficult work why shouldn't you feel nervous? It is the man who feels unduly nervous for the hundredth performance who is a bit unhealthy. Accept a reasonable degree of nervousness just as a doctor accepts the risk of infection or a policeman accepts night duty or a deep-sea fisherman accepts the wet and the cold.

Experience diminishes nerves, but there is no magic cure. Never touch wood. Beware of the parent who wants you to succeed because he or she failed. Beware of the teacher who lives by examination successes. Watch great performers and discover what they have in common, not how their eccentricities differ. Teach yourself nine-tenths of what you need to know and be grateful to your teacher for the other tenth.

Do all these things and you will attract more love and admiration than you deserve.

XIII

Accompanying

I found out about accompanying by doing it. What did I discover? Apart from sight reading, I discovered that the easiest way to accompany a song was to go along with the words rather than the melody. Foreign languages were a difficulty, but I could generally see my way through French, German, and Italian words without understanding them all, and Russian was fortunately rare.

There are no words in violin music, but I found that violinists kept stricter time than singers.

I enjoyed songs best. At one time I made the mistake of darting as soon as possible to the surface of the next note, lying in wait for the voice to arrive. It is true that this made me spot-on, but the process was unnatural, and I soon preferred to make my hand breathe with the singer. My hand listened for initial consonants. Hearing *th* it arrived easily and naturally on *thou*. A hiss directed it to *soul*, and a hum attracted it to *mine*.

I discovered that singers stayed in tune if my bass was firm and that they lasted through a long breath if I slightly accelerated my beats in the early part of the phrase. I knew how to give them the note after a silence or how to skip a beat to disguise a too early entry. I became very popular with singers.

I suppose I had to unlearn some of this low cunning when I later met serious singers of those great romantic songs called *lieder*, but as a boy I had learned to accept emotion. If a singer sang of jealousy and despair I played with jealousy and despair. Can *you* play with jealousy and despair? Many accompanists fail in this. Their only virtue—an important one—is that they do not hinder the singer. They discreetly accompany, hiding behind him and having an insufficient influence on the performance.

I preferred to make a serious contribution, but I never believed that a song is a share-and-share affair. Chamber music, yes—say, a violin and piano sonata—but in a song it is the singer who tells the story and I must tell it his way. In chamber music I take my bow as a matter of course: in a song I bow only if the singer invites me to.

Singers warmed the cockles of my heart. With experience I warmed theirs. Nowadays I am exasperated by the pupil who wants to play a Schubert Impromptu but has never accompanied *The Wanderer* or *Who is Sylvia?* And how often have I seen blank looks of non-understanding when I suggest that a Mozart slow movement must be played like a Mozart *aria* in an opera—for example, one of the songs sung by the Countess in *The Marriage of Figaro*.

Accompanying taught me to look ahead—often far ahead. While the hero, holding a top note, was picking up his sword, I was stealing a glance at the death of the villain.

I gave up accompanying in public because audiences will not accept an accompanist as a soloist. The public is sometimes mistaken about this, but many an accompanist is not bold enough to be a soloist; and many a soloist will not give way, as he should, to a singer. I knew I could hold an audience on my own; I knew that audiences were prejudiced against accompanists who play solos; so I was compelled to give up something that I could do rather well.

If this sounds like swank, always remember that a public performer needs to have a little vanity in his character.

XIV

Pianos and Pianists as They Used to be

Our skill has a history. A serious pianist spends an hour or two with a harpsichord and gets a better idea of how to play Bach suitably on the piano, even though a piano can never imitate a harpsichord. He seldom plays a veteran piano. The enthusiasts who make old instruments anew feel that there is good reason to make a perfect harpsichord: they are not so willing to make an imperfect piano, and only a very few early-type pianos are reproduced.

However, our 'perfect' piano has existed for several generations and we can learn from vintage recordings and from mechanical pianos how the great pianists played before we were born. In the days of the Pianola and other mechanical pianos there were a few very expensive 'reproducing pianos' that most uncannily played as though the ghost of the pianist were sitting on the piano stool. At the recording session, as the artist played, his every note was automatically marked on a roll of paper unwinding at a constant speed. A system of electrical contacts revealed the velocity of each hammer-throw and therefore the loudness of the note. From the recording piano the roll went to the cutting room and then to the reproducing piano. The artist listened, asked for a few small corrections, signed the roll, authorized its issue and took his money. Restored pianos together with collections of rolls are now in museums or in the hands of private enthusiasts. Gramophone companies have recorded the performances, obtaining better results than by re-issuing very old records.

Many of the 'great old boys' played with a freedom that strikes us as exaggerated, but perhaps the romantic composers expected this and would dislike our careful, respectful performances. When as a young man I heard Paderewski as an old man (returning to the concert platform after being Prime Minister of Poland) I was shocked by much that he did, but I was impressed by his romantic intensity and his hold over the audience. There was nothing businesslike about him: you were not there to make a cool judgment of his skill. Your proper response was to be mesmerized.

For me, he was much too fond of playing the left hand before the right, but I went home and experimented with this effect. I also experimented with playing right before left. I learned something valuable and permanent about *cantabile-rubato*.

Most of Paderewski's contemporaries went in for being great personalities. There was the eccentric Vladimir de Pachmann who could waste twenty minutes getting the position of the piano altered, the stool changed, the lighting reduced, while he chatted in broken English to the people in the front row. There were a great many elegant performers like Lhévinne who concentrated on pieces popularly known as war-horses— for instance a seemingly impossibly difficult arrangement of *The Blue Danube*. Far removed from these pianists there were a few like Busoni whose manner seemed to say 'You're not going to like this, but it will do you good', whereupon he would play Bach's *Goldberg Variations* and follow it up with Beethoven's *Hammerklavier* Sonata. And Rachmaninoff will be remembered as a composer long after his wonderful playing is forgotten.

Behind the pianists there were the teachers. In the history of piano teaching we have the composers of exercises like Clementi and Czerny. We find a great pianist like Liszt who was also a great composer. He gave free lessons to very talented pupils. There were famous teachers who drew talent to them like a magnet, particularly Leschetizky in Vienna, 'turning out' a long line of famous virtuosi. Some of his pupils say there was a Leschetizky 'method': others strenuously deny this.

There was certainly a Matthay Method. Matthay in London gave memorable lessons to many talented pupils and had some splendid things to say. Unfortunately his books are very confusing. They gave rise to a great deal of pretty-pretty, girlish playing, and when the reaction set in people forgot what was well worth remembering.

E   65

Today we live with tape-recorders and slow-motion cameras. They take down your faults in evidence against you but never tell you the cure. The fact that they have a limited value does not mean they should be ignored. Far too many teachers are content to teach what they were brought up to believe. The good teachers know that they have much to learn. They hope that the next generation of teachers will be better.

XV

Heavy Pianists, Light Pianists, and Jazz Pianists

Jazz pianists are a race apart. For a long time there was almost no communication between serious pianists and jazz pianists. It was understood that a jazzman would never play Brahms and a serious pianist would never play *When the Saints go marching in*. The great divide was so unbridgeable that when I first broadcast George Gershwin's *Rhapsody in Blue*, I did so anonymously for fear of damaging my serious reputation.

Nowadays the gulf is not so uncrossable, yet there are few travellers from one side to the other. Why?

The fact is: there is a total difference of approach. As a serious pianist I study the text and revere the composer. A jazz pianist often has no text and reveres players—players who improvise but can scarcely be called composers. The serious player goes in for noble sentiments. The jazz player expresses every emotion except noble sentiments. The serious player plays in a great variety of styles. The jazz player plays in his own style—the one he is famous for.

It is a rare pianist who can play for a recital club today and for a jazz club tomorrow.

Jazz players never seem to have been taught by anyone. Some had ordinary lessons when young, some are completely self-taught; they all picked up a jazz style, often by imitating recording artists. Recorded performances are sometimes used to dictate the music to a musician who can write what he hears, but very few of these 'transcriptions' are close to the originals. If you can find a faithful version you must still learn the style from a record or from skilled jazz players in the flesh. We serious pianists know full well that style varies from composer to composer, from place to place, from era to era, and we know better than to play Handel in the style of Debussy. Yet we are oddly reluctant to seek the style of a jazz piece.

Perhaps this is snobbery. Perhaps, however, the serious player is as different from the jazz player as an actor is from a cabaret artist—a really different sort of human being. I cannot be sure. Jazz is evolving, and more and more of it is being seriously composed. Modern music of other kinds is evolving and more and more of it is being left to chance, to improvisation.

*   *   *

The light pianist, as distinct from the jazz pianist has usually been seriously trained but has evolved into what show-business calls an *artiste* rather than an artist. He is an entertainer first and foremost, regarding the audience as much more important than the composer. He seldom plays music as it was written, he cuts out all development, he plays medleys of well known tunes. He usually abandons serious music. This does not seem to be true of orchestral players who think nothing of recording a television jingle on a Monday and Beethoven's Ninth Symphony on a Tuesday.

If my description of a light pianist sounds a little contemptuous I must add a tribute. The best sort of light pianist not only plays the piano, he plays the audience. Like a story-teller he seems to say 'D'you remember, ol' boy . . .' and, playing a tune of perhaps no great merit, he plunges a middle-aged man into a mood of the completest nostalgia. He can set young feet dancing and old heads nodding and reminds us all of holidays and parties and love affairs. Never forget that Johann Strauss the Younger was admired by almost every great composer of his era, and nearly all of them wrote waltzes.

*   *   *

The concert pianist usually begins as a gifted boy, ambitious and a bit obsessed by the piano. He is a mixture of shyness and vanity, not always what teachers call a 'well-adjusted' child, timid perhaps in some ways but bold in performance. Discovering that he has power over people he grows bolder as he grows older. When he grows up he may feel more courageous than some of his schoolfellows who have unaccountably changed from demon footballers into polite haberdashers.

I talk of boys, having been one. The girls must forgive me. They live in a man's world and must play an instrument designed for a man's hands. Some men talk of 'women pianists' as though they were not quite the real thing. This is nonsense. A great pianist is a great pianist.

The principal risk for concert-pianists is insecurity. You are selling a personal skill and can never quite ignore your many rivals who think they are as good as you. You know that, of two pianists equal in merit, one may make a fortune and the other be unable to pay the rent. You never, never become thick-skinned about criticism. You must travel, perhaps more than you want, to pursue success. You will be envied (is that always enviable?), and you will feel envy.

There will be times when you will be over-loud, too obviously in search of publicity, thoroughly bogus. Adding your fees together and subtracting your expenses you will worry about your old age. You will reflect that concert artists are soon forgotten and you will resent the existence of rivals whose success is a mystery to you.

Yet, given a little success, a pianist is a privileged person and would not willingly change his way of life.

Amidst all the difficulties you must never let your piano become a nagging wife or a mere business asset. Your piano is your sweetheart and I hope you stay in love for ever.

XVI

Interpretation and the Unlearning of Rules

Heavy pianists, light pianists and jazz pianists have their different ways of interpreting music. Interpreting. . . . Interpretation is a much-used word, but what does it mean?

Even the youngest young person has some idea of interpretation, perhaps suggested by a title. In Album for the Young, *The Poor Orphan* ('gently, darling,') is quite different from *Soldiers' March* ('keep in step, boy'). And titles continue to be important. Even the greatest pianist could not guess how to play Schumann's Carnaval if the titles were removed from all its small pieces. Be sure, however, that you understand titles in foreign languages. The French word *pathétique* does not mean pitiful: it has a nobler and grander meaning than pathetic. A nocturne is not a go-to-sleep piece. There may be dreamy passages suggesting a gondola under the moon, but nocturnes are passionate and amorous. Sometimes when a composer has been at a loss for a title he has called his three-minute piece *Prélude* though it is not a prelude to anything in particular. Scarlatti's Sonatas are nothing like the later classical sonatas: indeed they were originally called exercises. In Bach's Partitas you will find that the first of a set of pieces may be called *Ouverture* or *Sinfonie*. The three-part Inventions are also sometimes called *Sinfonia*. And the Italian Concerto has no orchestra, though the layout of the music suggests an affinity with, say, the Brandenburg concertos.

Titles, then, can be either revealing or deceptive.

The same can be true of marks of expression. They are not as simple as they seem. A great deal of what a teacher tells a very young child must later be unlearned or re-thought. And even a young child may discover that the two hands are seldom played at equal strength; while long notes must be loud enough to last their length, even in a soft piece.

But when the word Interpretation begins to have significance we must ask ourselves if marks of expression can mean something apart from their simple definitions. One of my favourite illustrations is to play—with equal force—the G at the top of the treble stave and the G at the bottom of the bass. Play them together and listen . . . holding them. After a few seconds the high note will have died away and you will hear only the low one.

Now play the top G with great force and the low one quite gently. Listen. In a few moments you will hear them living together amicably, well balanced.

What is that? *Forte* or *piano*? Do not expect a composer to mark the difference. He assumes you know what pianos are like.

Going on from there let us ask ourselves some more questions about soft notes in loud pieces and vice versa. Here are two examples of loud music in which the soft notes outnumber the loud ones.

Ex. 20

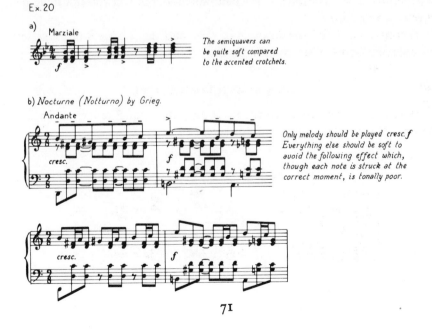

a) Marziale

The semiquavers can be quite soft compared to the accented crotchets.

b) *Nocturne (Notturno) by Grieg.*

Andante

Only melody should be played cresc. *f* Everything else should be soft to avoid the following effect which, though each note is struck at the correct moment, is tonally poor.

Another point about tone: always remember that a single high note *ff* can sound disagreeable even on a fine piano. A double octave passage, equally high and equally loud, can sound brilliant. And let me assure you that even a great pianist may play at less than full strength if he is confronted with a long, loud, fast, and difficult *étude*. Even *his* muscles if overtaxed might otherwise give out before the last page.

The judgement of softness is probably more difficult than the judgement of loudness. There are times when extreme softness, on the threshhold of silence, can make a wonderful effect, particularly on a very grand grand piano. Never forget, however, that softness is often a 'stage whisper'. Singing teachers are always talking about the sort of voice production that 'carries'. What they have in mind is that when Madam Butterfly or La Traviata is dying, her last gasp must be heard in the back row of the 'gods'. You, too, must hold the attention of the listener at the back of the hall. A merely obedient, diligent softness will seldom do the trick. There is a something that starts inside you and goes along your arm and through your fingers that gives the impression—to yourself as well as your audience—that you have entered the piano and come out again with a generous handful of tone. It is a contradiction, but can you not imagine a resounding softness?

Having considered the softness of *forte* and the loudness of *piano* let us re-define some other common terms.

CRESCENDO AND DIMINUENDO

Here are two examples. In the first, three *dims* equal one *cresc*. In the second, three bulges equal one squeeze.

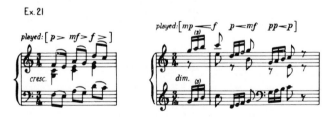

Ex. 21

Sometimes a composer's *dim* is, in a way, disobeyed because one thinks of how a bass singer or 'cellist might project the last few notes of a melody—as in Chopin's B minor Prelude (No. 6).

Ex. 22

Where a melody gets louder and louder, its accompaniment must also increase, but often to a lesser extent. There are some accompanying figures that can become 'exercisy' and boring at a *forte* level.

Always look at the distance between one sign and the next. *p cresc.* . . . . *f* is very different from *pp* < *ff*. In a long and gradual *cresc* the great danger is that you will be too loud too soon. And vice versa. In a long, gradual change be sure to start at a level of tone that will make the whole thing possible. There are teachers who say *cresc* means soft; *dim* means loud. They are talking about starting-levels, and it is often true that a *dim* begins with accent. Generally it is best to wait until you see the composer's sign before taking action, but sometimes coming events cast their shadow before.

ACCELERANDO AND RALLENTANDO

Not too fast, or too slow, too soon. Calculate and pay proper respect to the word *poco*. Headstrong pianists (and I hope you can sometimes be headstrong) tend to alter *poco* into *molto*. So, alas, do diligent and conscientious students. Remember your grammar. *Ritenuto* is more immediate than *ritardando*—slowed rather than slowing. And *allargando* may mean not only broadening the beat but enlarging your manner with a suggestion of increasing grandeur.

STACCATO

You can be so concerned with take-off as to spoil put-down. An effective staccato passage is often best done, not by taking off each note, but by pouncing down from a small height. Try playing a fast scale using only one finger and you will discover the right action and sensation. Try it with a weak finger and let that weak finger accept little hammer-blows from the arm.

Books on the theory of piano playing assert that there are three degrees of staccato.

Ex. 23

The *mezzo staccato*—slur and dot combined—is about right for most occasions, but the idea that the slash is *staccatissimo* compared with the dot is more than doubtful. A Haydn *Urtext* gives many more slashes than dots. It is hard to believe that Haydn is more staccato than Mozart.

A dot over the beat-notes in a continuing passage nearly always means a flick of accent, as in Beethoven's Sonata Pathétique.

Ex. 24

cresc.   *etc.*

CON BRIO

The usual answer in an examination is 'with vigour'. But *brio* is a kind of manly quality, the heroism of the handsome young tenor in a romantic opera. Play accordingly and remember that a girl can play the piano in a manly way just as a boy, meeting words like *Grazioso, capriccioso,* can ask his other self to produce a certain feminine grace.

CON PEDALE

'Syncopated' *legato* pedalling has already been explained. Long after the trick was known, composers and publishers went on with a deceptive notation. They showed the end of a pedalling by means of an asterisk and placed it too far to the left. If you wonder why they should have been so foolish, remember that traditions die hard. (Think of English spelling.) And now look at Chopin's pedalling as originally printed.

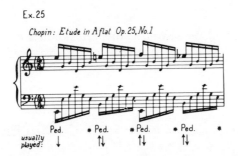

Ex. 25

Chopin: *Etude in A flat Op. 25, No. 1*

usually played:

Beethoven has some controversial pedallings that if literally obeyed may produce a great blur of sound. Did he really mean a great blur of sound, or was the result different on the pianos of his era, or was he too deaf to realize what was happening? On the whole I obey him . . . allowing for one or two half-secret adjustments.

I always like to see an Urtext based not only on a composer's manuscript but also on the first edition that was published after he corrected the proofs (and which may therefore be more correct than the manuscript). Let us learn what signs mean: also what they used to mean.

And talking of what signs used to mean we come to the . . .

SLUR

Children taught teaching-pieces are told, 'Play smoothly until you reach the last note and then take your hand off.' Unfortunately they often learn two more notions. One is that the hand should be snatched off as soon as possible. The other is that the last note should be 'shaded off'.

Instead of saying, 'Take your hand off the last note of a slur,' I would rather say, 'Put your hand on the first note, coming down from a small height.'

Ex. 26

As for shading off the last note, this can produce a ridiculous effect if the last note is on a first beat. A song makes this clear:

Ex. 27

My Bon-nie lies o - ver the   o - cean,   My Bon-nie lies o - ver the   sea ____

From this we may accept the general idea that there may be an accent on the final first-beat in a phrase. There will be exceptions, of course, rather particularly in 3-time. But if we change a waltz from 3/4 to 6/8 we shall see that the exception is more apparent than real.

Ex. 28

Chopin: Valse in C sharp minor Op. 64, No. 2

changed to 6/8

and now the slur shades off at a weaker beat.

Keep this in mind. In 3-time there is nearly always an alternation of stronger and weaker bars that would be clearer if notated in six. And make sure that you know whether the opening bar is strong or weak.

Ex. 29

Johann Strauss: The Blue Danube

The second bar is strong, where the long A begins.

If in doubt, experiment.

Now we come to a problem that editors attempt to solve and sometimes obscure. The slurs in classical music are not like those in teaching-pieces. To understand them, remember that Haydn, Mozart, and Beethoven were composers of symphonies. In those symphonies they often wrote slurs as bowing indications for string players. And they 'bowed' their piano pieces.

In a short run of notes their slurs often seem to end one note too soon. But if you think of the final note as having a different bow-direction you will realize that it has some slight degree of accent. A modern slur reaching to the last note may seem to show the length of a group, but it tends to rob the last note of accent.

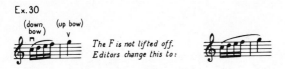

Ex. 30

(down bow) (up bow)

The F is not lifted off. Editors change this to:

When Mozart slurs an expressive phrase like this . . .

Ex. 31

I like to imagine the bow starting on F sharp, changing direction on B flat with slight emphasis, and again on C sharp, a final note that tugs on one's heart-strings. A slur over the whole thing has less meaning.

I cannot pretend that the thought of bowing will solve all problems. I have never been able to discover what Beethoven meant by his slurs in

77

the slow movement of Sonata Pathétique, and many editors have boldly altered them. Have *you* a solution?

Ex. 32

In performance I make this melody breathe as a singer would.

Two-note slurs usually follow the rule that the first of the two notes is accented. However, in Beethoven's Sonata in G, Op. 14, No. 2, you should, I think, obey the rule on one page and disobey it on another.

Ex. 33

PAUSE

If the music stops, *you* stop. Don't fidget or start preparing the next note too soon. Hold it! If there is a rest-pause, hold your hand (fingers relaxed) just above the stopping place. When it is time to re-start, go to the next position. In a really long silence you may put your hands on your knees and look thoughtful.

TEMPO

A speed-word like *allegro* or *lento* refers to the pace of the beats, not the pace of the notes. This being so there ought to be a clear difference between

$$\mathbf{c} \; \text{♩ ♩ ♩ ♩} \quad \text{and} \quad \mathbf{¢} \; \text{♩ ♩ ♩♩}$$
beat, beat beat beat   beat   beat

In theory the notes of the second example should move twice as quickly, if the beat is unaltered, since there are now two notes to the beat. In many cases this theory is obeyed in practice, but the rule is not strict. The most puzzling exception is the first movement of the 'Moonlight' Sonata where Beethoven's two minims (¢) seem so impracticable that many editors have rather impertinently printed four crotchets (c). However, to dodge the issue, you can avoid counting 1 2 3 4 and count 1 & 2 &. This may seem a mere 'get-out', but it does reveal something about the rhythm.

Learning a classical slow movement you may choose to count, say, four to a beat to make the time values exact. As you get nearer to performance-level, stop counting every little note. Feel the big beats. This helps to change mere time into rhythm. It is fairly true (there are no universal truths in interpretation) that the difference between time and rhythm is accent. And accentuation in all its variety is an art that consists of much more than obeying the printed accents. A printed accent makes a note stand out. The unprinted accents give life to rhythm.

XVII

The Interpretation of Time

The chapter on time values in your theory book makes it quite clear that twice two is four, and most people do not expect to interpret the twice times table. This, however, is something we must learn to do —with subtlety—but only after getting the time values exact. You must be able to read before you start reading between the lines.

Let us take some examples.

Ex. 34

Bach: French Suite No. 4 in Eb - the Courante

interpreted in this way:

Bach's ♪ in this case is played as a third of the beat

Bach: Bk. I of the 48, Fugue in D (No. 5)

usually played:

♪ becomes ♪ in both staves — an eighth of the beat

Beethoven 'Moonlight' Sonata

always played as:

♪ not a quarter but a sixth of the beat

In the dance music of the twentieth century the semiquaver after the dot is often played as a third of the beat. Indeed, dance music of any century and any country is hard to notate exactly. One must sense the swirls and swoops and lifts and stops that go with the music. For instance, Sarabandes and Tangos may seem far removed from one another but both depend on knowing the moment of *stop*.

Ex. 35

Handel: *Sarabande from Suite No. 7 in G minor*

(slow and grand)

Sarabandes often stop on the second beat and then resume movement. This suggestion does not apply to every Sarabande or every bar. I have chosen an obvious specimen.

Albeniz: *Tango in D Op. 165, No. 2*

Andantino

A stop on the dotted crotchet chords – not a pause. The dancer's movement halts.... and resumes.

Chopin, in his Mazurkas, often replaces a dotted note by a note-and-rest. The rest needs a good lift-off making the semiquaver late—very, very slightly. It makes the music airborne.

Ex. 36

Chopin: *Mazurka Op. 7, No. 1*

Vivace

The suggested fingering helps to ensure a good lift-off from each rest.

Waltzes sometimes need a lift-off from a second beat. At one time this trick-of-the-trade tended to be overdone by players searching for the Viennese style, but it has its moments not only in the Vienna of Strauss and Schubert, but in the Paris of Chopin. It helps to make a waltz 'sweep her off her feet'.

Ex. 37

Johann Strauss: 'Voices of Spring'

Chopin: Grande Valse Brillante Op. 18.

In interpreting time, remember how different a conductor's beats are from the tick of a metronome—watch the punch of this beat, the lift of that beat, and the swoop-along of others. Organize the beats, and realize that a minuet that begins a phrase on a 3 and ends on a 2 is not a mere 3-in-a-bar.

Ex. 38

Beethoven: Minuet in G

Rubato is a problem we met when discussing the Beauty-of-Tone Problem (Chapter IX). It is very important in certain kinds of romantic music. Equally important are the departures from arithmetical time that are so slight as not to be described as *rubato*. They are cunning, almost imponderable, and they make the audience say, 'What a beautiful sense of rhythm!'

ORNAMENTS

Many editions provide helpful footnotes in which trills and turns and suchlike are printed in full. Much of this work is expertly done and may be followed. There is, however, a limitation. The editor must choose whether to use semiquavers or demisemiquavers or whatever. Bach himself used demisemiquavers in his well-known table of ornaments. But are we to assume that every trill must be exactly counted? I readily admit that in many cases an orderly, sober, exact trill strikes us as being in good style, but we must not forget the very meaning of such words as ornaments and grace-notes. Does one count the flashes from the diamonds in a grand duchess's tiara or notate the trilling of her caged canary? In palaces and stately homes where ceilings were painted and furniture was full of inlay—in the royal opera house or the cardinal's chapel—the singers came with their expensive voices and shivered on an accent, and warbled through a long note, and lovingly transformed a mere cadence into an incredible cadenza, leaning on every *appoggiatura* (leaning-note) with the most delicate sensibility. Much of this was done without the composer's leave. He, sitting at his harpsichord, had to direct his orchestra in a way that would accommodate all these extravagances.

Cultivate a little scepticism about examination answers. Ex. 39 provides possible answers to several questions. Need a crushed note (*acciaccatura*) be very closely crushed when it has time available, as in a slow movement? Does a leaning-note take exactly half the value of its principal note, or should we quite literally lean on it and give it something more than exact arithmetic? An exactly timed group of fast notes to constitute an ornament can add glitter to a melody, but must an Alberti-bass go ticking along implacably?

Ex. 39

Haydn: Sonata in C (H. 16-35) Slow movement, bars 22-25.

More Haydn. What does it mean?

CADENZAS

In any passage printed without barlines and, perhaps, marked *ad libitum* or *a piacere*, always begin by practising the time values as they are. They do approximate to the truth even though the composer asks for freedom. You can then start to make a big thing of a big note or transform a rest into a profound silence. Beware of playing runs as though the real music had stopped and you were suddenly practising your scales. Begin the scale slowly . . . hurry . . . intensify . . . broaden out near the end. See what a fluttering pedal will do by way of adding brilliance without creating a blur. Mozart's Fantasia in D minor provides several examples, preparing you for concertos. Apart from the cadenzas, much of this piece is like a scene in an opera, full of anguish and disaster until good news in the major key comes near the end.

XVIII

The Harpsichord Problem

If you can, put your fingers on a harpsichord. Play a few simple phrases. If it is a two-manual instrument compare the sound on one keyboard with what you can obtain with the other using the lute stop. Enjoy the effect produced by octave-couplers and notice that when one finger is enabled to play an octave, the pressure has to be twice as strong.

You will find that quick notes come out with a *ping* and a clatter that might make you want to play similar notes staccato on a piano. Big chords, however, will have more duration than you might expect. Try a few ornaments. How distinct the notes are! Become accustomed to the absence of a sustaining pedal.

Slight accent is possible and this can be further suggested by playing the previous note staccato, but there is virtually no nuance or shading of tone. You play at one level of tone for so long; and then, by moving to the other keyboard or rearranging the stops (pedals), you play at another level—in 'terraced' tone.

How much of all this can be transferred to your piano playing? The trouble is that you may overload yourself with prohibitions. No pedalling. No nuance. No *cresc* or *dim*. In this way you will abandon all the advantages of the piano without enjoying such advantages of the harpsichord as two keyboards, octave couplers and the like.

When the harpsichord was replaced by the piano there were editors ready to sprinkle Bach's text with all sorts of pianistic signs. Czerny was one. His edition of the Forty-Eight is like a dish ludicrously full of pepper and salt, sugar and spice.

How, then, shall we solve this problem? Here are some suggestions.

Nearly all the quicker pieces seem to need harpsichordish qualities—a very crisp touch, distinct notes, almost no pedal, clear beginnings and endings to the shapes.

In slower pieces remember that the harpsichord was not the only *clavier*. The clavichord was the alternative. It was small. At its loudest it was still quiet. But it did have nuance and some degree of *cresc-dim*. And if you shook your finger while holding a note you could obtain a slight *vibrato*. The reason for this was that the string was pushed, not plucked. Perhaps, then, Bach's clavier music is not all bright and sparkling. Perhaps it can be intimately expressive. Remember this when a prelude is full of poignant harmonies—as, for example, Prelude No. 4 (C sharp minor) in Book I. Ask yourself which of the notes you would choose to linger on and play *vibrato* if you had a clavichord.

Bach's harmonies are sometimes ignored by pianists concentrating on his counterpoint. But his harmonies were extraordinarily bold and advanced, positively Wagnerian in places. It is true he never wrote an opera or a love song, but his music tells me that he was romantic and passionate to a degree probably not realized by friends and colleagues who knew him as pious and learned.

Once, at a musical conference, I heard the first fugue of the Forty-Eight played by a string quartet, expressively, just to see what it would sound like. I shall never forget how beautiful it was.

If this seems surprising let me remind you that much of Bach's choral music looks like his clavier music. Why not take that as a model? Listen to Crucifixion music. Then listen to one of the more joyful cantatas. Perhaps they may provide a clue. Even Bach's keyboard music may turn out to be a song without words.

In a long, wandering melody try to guess how a flautist would breathe.

Having said all this I must retreat a little and warn against allowing Bach to sound pretty-pretty. The third prelude in Book I is not, definitely not, a dance of the butterflies. In moments of intense feeling Bach is more likely to yearn after heavenly bliss than earthly joys. He is seldom sugary-sweet and never wrote a song about a girl's blue eyes.

What he did write was dance music. It was part of his job as a prince's Kapellmeister. Stern musicians sometimes assure me that music in the dance-forms need not sound like dance music. I wonder. Chopin's waltzes sound like waltzes even when they are played much too fast or too slow for the ballroom. Is there no dance rhythm in a French Suite? It is true that I cannot always feel a dance-impulse in an Allemande or a Loure and must be content to play either of them as an Invention. But there are surely Minuets and Sarabandes and Gavottes and Gigues that could possibly have inspired Prince Charming and Cinderella to take the floor—always remembering to preserve his highness's dignity.

Not many pianists venture to use the *notes inégales* that some authorities assure us are appropriate in dance music. Pairs of quavers, so they say, need not be played in even twos. Perhaps a Sarabande could be interpreted. . . .

Ex. 40

Bach: *Sarabande from French Suite in D minor*

may have been interpreted, less solemnly as:

Only a very experienced musician would dare to use an Urtext and find phrasing for himself. A Young Person must rely on teacher or a 'standard edition'. But he may well wonder how so-called authorities decide the length of a slur that Bach himself never wrote.

A couple of examples may indicate how inspection of the text may provide a clue.

Ex. 41

Bach: *The 48 Bk.1 No. 2*

The second phrasing, because, later, one finds a leap that would make the first unlikely.

Bk.1 No.18

The slur ends on D sharp because Bach later uses the remaining notes separately.

The experts will never agree. Every now and again a new pundit attracts disciples. But there is one obvious course of action open to you. Borrow several recordings of one piece. Of course they will differ. But pay attention to what they have in common.

XIX

The Sonata Problem

‘Do you study Form?’
   ‘Yes, with Mr. X.’
  ‘Does it influence your piano playing?’
  ‘Should it?’
This is a true report of a conversation with a pupil of mine some years ago.

There was a time when students were instructed to look out for the second subject of a sonata and play it *poco meno mosso*, even if nothing of the kind was marked, just to show that a new event had begun. Nowadays pianists fear that this will destroy the unity of conception. Either way, we do need to acknowledge form. But how?

Let us start with the proposition that a long movement may tell a story. I am not thinking of the sort of programme music that can be put into words or illustrated by a picture. I am suggesting that there is a succession of happenings and events and that these may influence our playing even in the absence of instructions.

There are two approaches. One is to cast yourself in the role of composer, as though you yourself were ‘telling’ us the first thing and then thinking about what to ‘say’ next. The other is not dissimilar and consists of a kind of translation:

con brio—‘head high and full of courage, he . . .’
dolce e cantabile—‘thinking of all he held dear, he . . .’
minore (p subito)—‘assailed by melancholy fears, she . . .’
maggiore—‘refreshed by the arrival of good news, they . . .’

These phrases do not tell a specific story, but they do remind us that musical character and human character are similar. It may be very unsophisticated to think that everything minor is sad and everything major is gay, but an unsophisticated notion may be true for much of the time. To go straight past a change of mode as though nothing had happened is generally not a good idea. If you respond in such a way as to make a change of mode a change of mood you may decide to do so with subtlety; but changes of mode, changes of key, changes of pitch do mean something. If operatic villains have bass voices and heroes are tenors; if terror is often accompanied by a diminished seventh chord (strings tremolo); if a flute solo suggests pastoral peace; if a flourish of trumpets is a declaration of war; if most duets are love duets, ask yourself if there isn't some suggestion of voices and orchestra and stirring events in your sonata.

It must be said again that Mozart's sonatas were by the composer of *Don Giovanni* and Beethoven's by the composer of *Fidelio*.

I am not trying to persuade you that every sonata should be played operatically, but I do wish to bring the music to life. An endless succession of carefully practised details may not achieve this. Be bold. There are some people who would like to scale-down our performances on the grounds that earlier pianos were not like our concert-grands. Maybe: but earlier drawing-rooms were not like our vast concert halls. And, in any case, a Beethoven sonata may be similar in style to a Beethoven symphony with its brass and timpani.

No doubt exaggeration is bad, but timidity is worse.

XX

The Age of Song

Schubert, Schumann, and Brahms were all great song writers. The world has rather forgotten that Liszt wrote many songs. It knows that Chopin wrote only a few. However, let us apply to all their piano music the title that Mendelssohn invented—Songs without Words.

A singer must learn to shape his words and 'produce' the voice. Something of this can find its way into your mind and understanding if you will accompany songs seriously. (See Chapter XIII.)

Somehow we must be able to suggest that a piano has voice production. We know in cold fact that hammers hit strings, but somehow we must make sounds emerge as though without percussion. Fortunately a fine piano is a marvellous piece of technology that seems to respond, almost in human fashion, to gestures. These invite it to utter all kinds of words in a language that has no dictionary. There is an element in a pianist's touch that is very like a conductor's mime.

Some people argue that piano hammers can never respond to mime. Hammers can only be flung at the strings at a certain velocity, producing the consequent loudness. Other pianists persuade themselves that in some mysterious way a hammer can arrive on the string with some characteristic that is not mere velocity. My engineering sense tells me that the first argument is right, but I always play as though the second one were true. In art as in life one has to recognize that some notions, if not scientifically true, are *as if* true, and I am not talking of falsehoods, delusions, and superstitions. One plays romantic music as if the piano were human and could be cajoled by embracing a phrase or squeezing a chord or caressing a note, or passing one's hand over a musical shape as art-lovers stroke a piece of sculpture, sensing as well as seeing the contours.

At the same time one must be almost coldly aware of one's muscular behaviour. And here is a detail from Liszt's famous *Liebestraum*.

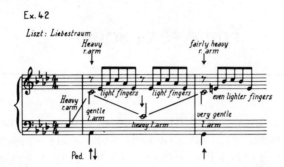

Ex. 42

And that's only the half of it! Common sense on the one hand; sensibility on the other; you can never have too much of either.

XXI

Strength and Agility

If you are ambitious you will need strong muscles and swift thought. What about exercises and studies?

Many of the old books of studies were over-written. Any and every exercise had to be played in twelve major and twelve minor keys—a chilling prospect. To ignore such things entirely, however, might suggest that you are not serious about piano playing.

One thing is sure: scales and arpeggios (see Chapter VII) are important. Many people 'know' them well enough not to get a fail-mark in an examination, but managing to reach pass standard is not good enough. Fingers can be strengthened by playing from a very soft note to a very loud one very quickly. When a pair of notes has been played like this you stop and make sure that every finger, other than the holding-finger, is relaxed (see Ex. 43). This can be remarkably effective. I have seen infirm players 'firmed up' in a few weeks of serious work.

If books of exercises chill your blood, why not learn pieces that are exercises turned into music? A very good example for the older Young Person is Beethoven's 32 Variations in C minor.

Cultivate memory so that you can give real attention to what happens on the keyboard—what happens between spine and finger-tip. Do not be afraid to raise your elbow to shoulder height before a well-aimed, well-timed descent to the tone-target. Be aware of your contact with the piano stool and know how to transfer your weight from the left haunch to the right as you move from the bottom end of the keyboard to the top. Have an active pedal-foot, but keep contact. Never stamp on the pedal. Address yourself to the keys but avoid a sniff-the-keys crouch.

Mindless drudgery may be a bad thing, but sheer repetition does have value. A cluster of notes played fifty times may only take ten minutes of practice time.

If you practise a fast passage slowly there is no point in stamping your way through it in the spirit of a child taking a nasty medicine to do him good. Pretend that it is slow music to be played with a proper respect for every sound. This is often a good approach to speed and power, but it will not work in every case. Every child knows that there is no slow way to hop or jump. An athlete jumping over hurdles, or a diver going off the top board with two somersaults before reaching the water, cannot go through the motions slowly. There are some actions that can only be tried—and tried again and again—at speed.

In Ex. 43 I give a number of suggestions. Practise them when you are alone in the house and the neighbours have gone shopping.

Ex. 43

STRENGTH AND AGILITY

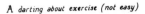

In practice, play
the treble group
very evenly and
place the chords
as follows ~ as
grace-notes
before B♭ and G.

A darting about exercise (not easy)

.... in the mirror (don't neglect left arm skills)

Advanced athletics for the ambitious.

Based on Chopin's Etude in G sharp minor Op. 25, No. 6

Based on Liszt's 'Feux Follets'. The treble part is Liszt's. The left hand here is a mirror version.

95

XXII

Take a Bow

To play to people you need a little vanity. Not conceit. Conceit consists of kidding yourself. Vanity is the desire to display a truly existent beauty or talent or persuasiveness. I had it when I was a clever little boy. If I went anywhere and nobody asked me to play I was affronted.

Fortunately at the age of about twelve I was given some serious and intelligent instruction in platform behaviour—the modest small bow, the slightly deeper bow on being recalled, the deeper and courtly bow (hand on the end of the keyboard) in response to tumultuous applause, the smiling look at the audience that seems to say, 'Ladies and Gentlemen, do you really want an encore?'

Deportment can never be standardized. We all learn to recognize that some very great pianists have peculiarities and mannerisms, but you may as well make a good image. I know that Mr. X sits very low, and Monsieur Y sits huddled up, and Herr Z grunts every time he encounters an accent, but if ever you see a really old pianist who continues to play marvellously you may depend upon it that he has a wonderfully easy action.

Remember that highly skilled actions confer beauty on you. The romantic novelist's picture of an ugly little man transformed by the way he plays an instrument has more than a grain of truth in it.

Conversely I have seen pretty girls lose their attractiveness by 'emoting' too much. (This is seldom a masculine fault.) They wriggle on each note, yearn over every chord, and hang their heads for every *pianissimo*. This nearly always interferes with agility, and a seemingly graceful *lento* gives

96

way to a sluggish *allegro*. Their male rivals sometimes play with a fine, athletic vigour in an *allegro* but look uncomfortably inhibited in an *andante cantabile*.

Some teachers and students use tape-recorders in order to judge a performance. I sometimes wish they would use a cine-camera. They might be embarrassed by what they see.

Gesture is part of piano playing but avoid a bogus expansiveness. How often have I seen someone over-prepare a chord, playing it very cautiously, then throwing the hands off with a great air of confidence. I am much more impressed by a confident arrival than by a demonstrative departure.

Trust yourself. A piano is a strange creature. It is like a lion. Never let it think that the lion-tamer is afraid. If you prefer to think of yourself as the lion (or lioness) regard the piano as a lioness (or lion) and be wild, tender, and loyal.

Nobly animal and profoundly human you will be glad you 'learned the piano'.

Index

Accent, 21, 43, 47
Accompaniment, 25, 40, 42, 62–3
Action (piano mechanism), 16
Albeniz, 81
Announcing (titles), 60
Arm touch, 41
Arpeggios, 18, 34–6, 94

Bach, 18, 46, 47, 49–51, 55, 58, 64, 65, 70, 80, 85–8
Barlines, 19–20
Beat, 21
Beethoven, 17, 41, 45, 47, 58, 65, 68, 74, 75, 77–80, 82, 90, 93
Brahms, 67, 91
Busoni, 65

Cadenza, 84
Cantabile, 40, 65
Caprice, 25
Chopin, 17, 24–5, 46, 51, 55, 58, 73, 75–6, 81–2, 86, 91, 95
Clavichord, 86
Clementi, 65
Counterpoint, 50
Counting (time), 20–2
Czerny, 65, 85

Dampers, 11–13, 44
Debussy, 68
Design, 49–51

Ear (playing by), 19, 57
Elbow, 30
Escapement, 11
Etude, 46, 55, 72

Fall, 10
Faust, 17, 57
Finger action, 28–36
Fingering, 52–6
Forearm action, 29
French time names, 22
Fugue, 18, 49–51, 58

Gershwin, 67
Gigue, 47
Gounod, 17
Grand (piano), 11, 15
Grieg, 71

Hammer (*see* Action)
Handel, 68, 81
Hand-shape, 33
Hand-touch, 29
Harmonics, 15
Harpsichord, 64, 85–8
Haydn, 22, 74, 77
Hopper, 12

Improvisation, 67–8
Intermezzo, 25

Interpretation, 41, 70–80
Invention (Bach), 49–51

Jazz, 57, 67

Keys, 10–11
Klavarskribo, 20

Legato, 25, 28, 34, 42
Legatissimo, 44
Leschetizky, 65
Lhévinne, 65
Lieder, 62
Liszt, 18, 38, 47, 55, 65, 92, 95

Matthay, 65
Melody in F, 17
Memory, 59–61
Mendelssohn, 17, 91
Minuet, 18
'Moonlight' Sonata, 17, 41, 80
Mozart, 18, 47, 63, 77, 84, 90

Nervousness, 61
Nocturne, 24, 46, 70
Notation, 19–20

Octaves (playing of), 38
Orchestra, 47, 90
Ornaments, 55, 83–4
Overstringing, 10
Overtones, 15

Pachmann, 65
Paderewski, 65
Partials, 15
Part-playing, 49–51
Pedals, 11–14, 26
Phrasing, 24–7, 75–8
Pianists (famous), 64–6
Piano (mechanism), 9–14
Pianola, 64

Pitch, 15
Practice, 17–18, 52–6, 93–4
Prelude, 25, 70

Rubato 45–6, 83

Saint-Saëns, 60
Scales, 18, 34, 94
Scarlatti, 70
Schubert, 63, 82, 91
Schumann, 59, 70, 91
Sinding, 17
Sight-reading, 19–23
Singers, 62–3
Sonatas, 58, 89–90
Songs without Words, 25, 86
Soundboard, 11, 15
Staff (stave), 20
Staccato, 34
Stravinsky, 18
Stool (piano), 39
Strauss (Johann), 68, 77, 82
Strings, 9–11
Subject (fugue), 51

Tchaikovsky, 17
Technique, 52–6
Time-names, 22
Tone, 40–9
Tre Corde, 13
Trill, 55, 83
Twinkle, twinkle little star, 24

Upright (piano), 11, 15
Una Corda, 13, 39

Vamp-bass, 57
Vibrations, 11, 15
Voice (in counterpoint), 49–51

Wrist-action, 38, 42
Waltz, 47, 68, 82